HIDDEN HISTORY
of
CHAPEL HILL

HIDDEN HISTORY

of

CHAPEL HILL

Brian Burns

THE
History
PRESS

Published by The History Press
Charleston, SC
www.historypress.com

Front cover: Committee for Open Business March on May 25, 1963. Roland Giduz Photographic Collection #P0033, North Carolina Collection Photographic Archives, Louis Round Wilson Special Collections Library, University of North Carolina at Chapel Hill.
Back cover: Photo by author.

First published 2023

Manufactured in the United States

ISBN 9781467153553

Library of Congress Control Number: 2022950060

Notice: The information in this book is true and complete to the best of our knowledge. It is offered without guarantee on the part of the author or The History Press. The author and The History Press disclaim all liability in connection with the use of this book.

In memory of Leven Browne.

CONTENTS

ACKNOWLEDGEMENTS

When I first decided to write this book, I was determined to include Jim Wallace's compelling photos of the desegregation battle in Chapel Hill. A year or so later, sadly, I learned that Jim had died in Florida at the age of seventy-seven and that his large photo collection hadn't yet been archived. I tracked down Stephen J. Fletcher, an archivist at UNC's Wilson Special Collections Library. He explained that Jim's photos were expected to come in-house—he just didn't know when. Stephen was a selfless miracle worker. To expedite the process, he voluntarily traveled to Florida to pick up the negatives from Jim's widow, Joleen, and buckled down in the cataloging process. I'm eternally grateful to him for going beyond the call of duty and keeping me posted on his progress. Of course, I owe a huge thanks to Joleen for gifting Jim's photo collection in the first place.

UNC's Special Collections Department was incredibly generous in sharing these and dozens of other historic photos. Thanks go to Matt Turi, Jason Tomberlin, Sarah Carrier and Tim Hodgdon for their exhaustive research and duplication services. They were quick to honor my requests and always kept their cool.

A special nod goes to the Chapel Hill Historical Society. I thank Tom Jepson and Julie Wiker for their active interest in my project. And Richard Ellington suggested a topic to round out my book: the 1960s-era Speaker Ban Law.

I must also recognize Georgann Eubanks, executive director of the Paul Green Foundation. She culled through their photo collection and generously shared a rare image of the famed twentieth-century dramatist and civil rights activist. We bonded over our admiration for him.

The State Archives of North Carolina was another treasure trove. Thanks to Katherine Crickmore, I got my hands on some intriguing Hargrave family papers from the mid-1800s. Other archivists connected me with several historic images, one of them a drawing by a UNC student from the late 1700s.

To my surprise, I had some major computer issues during this project. I would have really been stuck if it wasn't for my good friend Chris Schubert. She often helps me with her technological superpowers. I should probably put her on retainer.

I extend a big thank-you to my editor, Kate Jenkins. Not only was she always encouraging, kind and professional, but she also exhibited incredible patience in the face of protracted delays.

Of course, a simple thank-you doesn't cut it for my spouse, Judd Proctor. His support never flagged. To clear my calendar for writing, he cooked, washed dishes and did the laundry—all without a single complaint. He also made a great sounding board. And more than once, his one-in-a-million sense of humor really saved the day. I certainly wouldn't be the person I am without him.

INTRODUCTION

In the 1960s, while I was growing up in Chapel Hill, the town was embroiled in controversy. Of course, I couldn't see past my Lincoln Logs and little red fire engine. I was born in the midst of a nasty, thirteen-year fight over fluoridating the local water supply. It pitted university officials against millionaire capitalist John Sprunt Hill and eccentric tax accountant Manning Simons. Hill called fluoridation a big hoax, and Simons held up the process in the courts. My father, a dentist in private practice, joined a group of citizens advocating fluoridation. The machinery finally got up and running in February 1964—one of my father's proudest moments.

In February 1960, when I was just two months old, students at the all-Black Lincoln High School picketed downtown lunch counters to protest segregation. In this instance, I'd bet my father sided with the segregationists. From the comfort of our black Naugahyde sofa, he watched archconservative Jesse Helms spew his venom on WRAL-TV in Raleigh. I didn't understand my father. I still don't. And he's been gone for nearly fifty years.

But he was hardly alone in his attitudes. Chapel Hill has a legacy of racism and white supremacy. UNC couldn't have opened in 1795 without slave labor and an infusion of slave-derived wealth. The university catered to the sons of aristocratic slaveholders. In the 1850s, when a UNC professor mildly criticized slavery, students burned him in effigy. After the Civil War broke out in 1861, a crowd of white Chapel Hillians raised a home-stitched Confederate flag and proclaimed the sanctity of slaveholding. Chapel Hillians were outraged in the 1870s, when the university's president talked of enrolling Black students. And in 1963 and 1964, the Board of Aldermen voted down a nondiscrimination ordinance.

Our Hillcrest Circle rancher was on "Strowd Hill," my father told me. Honestly, I didn't care enough about history to ask what that meant. But eventually, I became a convert. I dug through everything I could find about the 1,200-acre Strowd Plantation, from its late-1700s origins to its complete transformation today. I entered the world of Hardy Morgan, a wealthy Continental army veteran who grew tobacco in today's Glen Lennox area; escaped slave, Tom Morgan, who was shot by a posse and sent south; and the plantation's namesake, Robert Strowd, who was vital to Chapel Hill's prosperity, growth and image. Another standout was the revered 425-pound veterinarian Sim Nathan. In 1947, he opened a popular juke joint with carhops on East Franklin Street called the Curve Inn.

The town's past is chock-full of fascinating characters, if you just keep your eyes open. Adelaide Walters, the town's first female alderman and a world-class bird-watcher, worked tirelessly to help Chapel Hill live up to its promise. In her free time, she taught 1950s housewives how to break free of their apron strings and become community leaders. She also helped keep track of local bird species. In fact, she did so much charity work, I wondered when she slept.

Then there was Black high schooler Harold Foster. A pioneer in Chapel Hill's desegregation movement, he fought for three long years to bring his race the dignity it so desperately deserved. He and his fellow activists were willing to die for the cause of justice and racial equality. Some of them almost did.

My research felt more like a treasure hunt. Paul Green's name kept popping up. I already knew he was a famous playwright who developed Greenwood. But I was impressed by his deep moral convictions. He always made time for a righteous cause, whether it was social justice, nuclear disarmament, academic freedom or the town's growth and progress. He spoke truth to power.

If you're relatively new to Chapel Hill, I hope this book opens your eyes.

If you're an old-timer, I hope it triggers a special childhood memory. Maybe that's piling into the family's '57 Chevy to see a Doris Day movie at the Valley Drive-In on the bypass. Exploring the woods and stumbling upon Paul Green's cabin. Standing wide-eyed on Franklin Street in the cold, waiting for Santa Claus to parade by. Or sitting on a stool at the Dairy Bar counter, digging into that mile-high hot fudge sundae. Whatever it is, enjoy.

The Strowd Plantation

Past, Present and Future

At the same time and place…I will sell a valuable Female Servant,
who is an experienced cook, and her two Children.
—*Auction notice,* Hillsborough Recorder, *May 23, 1844*

During the Roaring Twenties—an era of jazz, flappers and Model T Fords—the 1,200-acre Strowd Plantation was ripe for development. Its hills and dales had witnessed a dizzying array of dramas. A male slave on the lam, for example, bloodied by a gun-toting posse. A wealthy planter, cheered for donating hundreds of acres to establish a groundbreaking university. Starved and ragged Confederate troops, hobbling in retreat. A promising young woman, struck down by a flu pandemic. As we'll see, most of the farm was transformed into residential neighborhoods for UNC's swelling ranks of brilliant professors and their families. But it was a long and tortuous journey, plagued by conflict, tragedy and ruin.

The saga begins shortly after the Revolutionary War, when Continental army veteran Hardy Morgan received two land grants from the State of North Carolina. He established a contiguous 980-acre plantation. It included today's Hillcrest Circle, Davie Circle, Glendale and parts of Greenwood, Glen Lennox and the Finley Golf Course area. Four hundred acres of the plantation—lying in a fertile plain along today's Little Creek—were ideal for cultivating cash crops like tobacco, cotton, wheat and corn. The hilly portions were suited only for timberland.

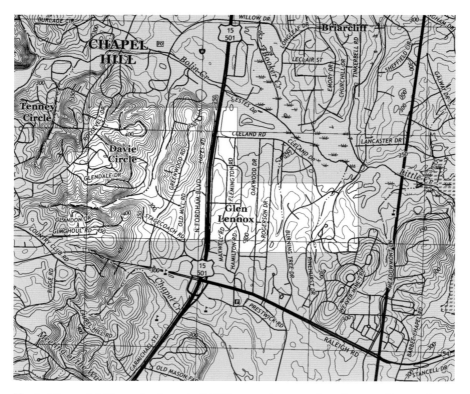

Hardy Morgan's 640-acre land grant of 1784, set against a modern-day map. Just south of the eastern portion was his irregular-shaped 340-acre land grant of 1788, with the old Raleigh Road running through. Records are sketchy about the latter's boundaries. *Map created by author, using U.S. Geological Survey.*

Running through Morgan's plantation was the old Raleigh Road, predecessor of Highway 54. It facilitated the transport of crops to market. As we might expect, Morgan used slave labor. His mother deeded him four slaves in 1780, and by 1790, he owned at least nine more. As a distinguished member of the landed gentry, his wealth, power and status relied on the institution of slavery.

As if Hardy Morgan didn't have enough property, he inherited hundreds of acres from his father, Mark Morgan. That included the former site of a log church, New Hope Chapel. It gave Chapel Hill its name.

In 1789, the year George Washington became president, the North Carolina General Assembly approved the bill for a public university. By late 1792, university trustees had fourteen sites under consideration. Hardy Morgan and other Orange County aristocrats pledged land donations for the campus, provided that New Hope Chapel Hill won the contest. The naturally beautiful area was at a convenient crossroads. The trustees confirmed their obvious choice that December and planned to lay off "a Town adjacent thereto." The enterprising Hardy Morgan fueled the ambitious scheme. He built a sawmill on Bolin Creek, about two hundred yards west of today's East Franklin Street.

In 1791, Morgan sold the 225-acre "Old Chapel Tract" to Christopher Barbee, one of the area's wealthiest land- and slaveholders. In turn, Barbee donated 221 acres of this property to the university.

In the sultry summer heat of 1793, slaves began clearing land for the campus. On August 10, as the Building Committee was marking off sites for the university buildings, it discovered a major oversight. A wedge of Hardy Morgan's land ran into the heart of the planned campus. Luckily, it was a problem money could fix. The Board of Trustees paid him $200 for an eighty-acre tract encompassing today's Coker Arboretum, Alderman Hall and Battle Park Pavilion. He granted old-growth pine timber rights to friend James Patterson, the planner-contractor for the East Building (now Old East). No doubt, the lumber was milled at Morgan's former sawmill, which Patterson purchased thirdhand that fall.

Apparently, Hardy Morgan's old-growth pine was used for the East Building's framing and roof shingles. *Courtesy of the State Archives of North Carolina.*

One of Chapel Hill's defining moments arrived on October 12, 1793. Culminating a solemn, Masonic parade, the university's moving spirit, William Richardson Davie, laid the cornerstone for the East Building. Reverend Samuel E. McCorkle, a staunch advocate of education, delivered the oration. He said, "The advancement of learning and science is one great means of ensuring the happiness of mankind." Next came the auctioning of lots that would constitute the village of Chapel Hill. Hardy Morgan was the highest bidder on a wooded, two-acre lot at the northwest corner of today's Franklin and Henderson Streets. He paid $150 but sold it the next year.

In early 1795, UNC became the nation's first state university to open its doors. By that June, it boasted forty-one male students. Its future, however, was anything but certain. So was its funding.

In 1796, Hardy Morgan honored his pledge, donating 125 acres to the university. The tract encompassed today's Kenan Stadium, Carmichael Auditorium, Cobb Dormitory and the old Chapel Hill Cemetery. With this philanthropic gesture, he surely hoped to bring prosperity and renown to the county and state. Besides, as the "seat of public enlightenment," the university could increase the value of his broad acres.

Sadly, he didn't live to see any of it happen. He died on April 17, 1797, at the age of fifty-three. His "beloved son," Lemuel Morgan, inherited half of the plantation and in 1811 purchased the other half. "One of nature's noblemen," he followed in his father's footsteps as a planter and land speculator. As such, he bought and sold many slaves.

In the early 1840s, Lemuel Morgan's luck ran out. Amid a major recession and a sharp decline in cotton prices, he found himself in deep debt. He owed hefty sums to the Bank of Cape Fear, the state's Literary Fund and friend William Barbee. Adding insult to injury, he guaranteed surety for merchant and Whig legislator Nathaniel J. King, who fled the state with public funds. Sheriff Ilai Nunn planned to auction off Lemuel Morgan's plantation and fifteen "valuable" slaves: Maria and her five children, Andrew, Bill, Ben, Sarah and Francis; Lucy and her two children, Mary and Haywood; as well as Charlotte, Sam, Stephen, George, Nelson and Tom.

On March 20, 1843, a public auction was held at Lemuel Morgan's plantation. The land didn't sell, but demand was high for the slaves. A slave trader purchased Tom Morgan, intent on selling him south. Tom couldn't bear the thought of a worse fate. He escaped. He hid in a rock outcropping about 325 yards southwest of today's intersection of Fordham Boulevard and Estes Drive. Former UNC president Kemp Plummer Battle recalled the lurid tale:

One of [Lemuel Morgan's] *slaves, Tom, having been bought by a trader who designed to carry him to the Southwest for sale, ran away and for several years had two hiding places, one…in a very thick copse of wood near his old master's residence, under the lee of overhanging rocks. Rough boards leaning against the rocks made a dismal shelter from the rain. There seemed to be little desire to molest him until he began to break into the stores of the village in search for meat. Then a posse was summoned for his capture. Marching through the forest at regular intervals—a process known as "beating the woods"—the men aroused him from his lair, and, on his refusal to stop when commanded, he was shot in the legs, captured and then sent south for sale.*

Trust Sale

OF VALUABLE LAND & SLAVES.

BY virtue of a deed of trust executed to me by Lemuel M. Morgan, on the 12th March, 1842, duly recorded and registered, I will proceed to sell to the highest bidder, on the premises, or Friday the 7th day of June next, (the day after the annual commencement of the University,) the valuable Tract of Land on which the said Lemuel M. Morgan now resides, containing nine hundred and thirty five acres, more or less. There is no difficulty in pronouncing this to be among the most fertile and valuable tracts of land in the county of Orange; and there are in the state few residences combining equal advantages of health, beauty of situation, contiguity of good society, and a literary institution of high character. The tract corners within a few hundred yards of the village of Chapel Hill, and includes about four hundred acres of excellent low grounds on Bolden's creek. The Dwelling House is handsomely situated about a mile from the village, and is, together with a good Barn, Kitchen, Dairy, and other houses, in a good state of repair.

At the same time and place, and for the same purposes, I will sell a valuable Female Servant, who is an experienced cook, and her two Children.

The terms, which will probably be accommodating at least in part, will be made known on the day of sale. The title is undoubted, but of course I convey as trustee only.

ILAI W. NUNN, *Trustee.*

Chapel Hill, april 8.   20—

After Lemuel Morgan's failed land auction in 1843, another attempt was scheduled for June 7, 1844. Hillsborough Recorder, *May 23, 1844.*

On June 7, 1844, the 935-acre plantation finally sold. Paying $4,300 was Jesse Hargrave, who owned Chapel Hill's leading general store on East Franklin Street. Jesse had arrived in the village bankrupt just nine years earlier. A contemporary described him as "an exceptionally prudent and careful man of business." His beautiful new wife, Margaret, came from the wealthy Barbee family (her grandfather was the largest contributor of land to the university). "An excellent woman, with a head for business," Margaret "materially assisted her husband's prosperity." She and Jesse had three children, Mary (born prior to marriage), Fred and Robert. The family slaves "worked in the house and yard and garden," said Fannie McDade, born a slave on the plantation in 1861. That suited her "people," she claimed, because "Mr. Jesse didn't raise crops and the servants didn't have field work to do." Entirely true or not, the farm was a massive slave operation. They kept large herds of hogs, sheep and cattle supplying milk, beef, pork and wool. The plantation house stood just northwest of today's intersection of Greenwood and Houston Roads, overlooking a broad, fertile plain. Nearby stood slave cabins, a barn, a smokehouse and an apple orchard.

An 1860 photo of the Hargrave home in the center of the village, near today's 103 East Franklin Street. By then, it was being used as a boardinghouse. *From* Incidents by the Way.

Jesse Hargrave purchased another large house on Franklin Street close to his store. When Chapel Hill was incorporated in 1851, he was named one of five commissioners to help "regulate" the growing village. In time, his great-grandson William R. Kenan Jr. would donate a football stadium to UNC.

On June 11, 1854, just six days after writing his will, Jesse Hargrave died. The *Fayetteville Observer* lamented the loss of "a valuable and much respected citizen." His wife inherited the house in the center of town. Interestingly, nine-year-old Fred inherited the plantation, and five-year-old Robert inherited the dry-goods store. Jesse's slaves were to be hired out "in order to secure them good masters and kind treatment."

In the late 1850s, the North and South became increasingly divided over the slavery issue. Even Chapel Hill was rooted in slavery. The village's prosperity depended on it.

THE NATION QUAKED ON April 16, 1861, when Republican president Abraham Lincoln called for seventy-five thousand volunteers to crush the rebellion in the South. Four days later, a crowd of white Chapel Hillians gathered to raise a Confederate flag sewn by the ladies of the village. They had stitched on a star symbolizing North Carolina, even though it hadn't yet joined the Confederacy. Several gentlemen delivered orations, insisting that the state do just that. Invoking the "rights of the slaveholder," lawyer Samuel F. Phillips proclaimed that Lincoln and his advisers "must be resisted even unto blood." The University Blues fired two salutes. Taking his turn on the soapbox, UNC president David L. Swain asserted that if every man in the South shouldered his musket, Mr. Lincoln would realize the South's invincibility and back down.

Within a few days, students began leaving Chapel Hill at the rate of eight to ten a day to join the Confederate army. On April 22, 1861, a group of area men not associated with the university met at Chapel Hill and enrolled for six months of active service. One of them was twenty-eight-year-old farmer and slaveholder William F. Strowd, destined to become a major figure in Chapel Hill. Most volunteers believed the war would be brief and decisive.

FOUR HORRIFIC YEARS LATER, the Confederate troops—decimated by war wounds and disease—were short on food, clothing and supplies. On April 9, 1865, General Robert E. Lee surrendered his Army of Northern Virginia.

On April 14, Confederate general Joe Wheeler's cavalry retreated through the village. A guest at the Hargrave plantation, Zoa Ann Long, took her two-year-old son by the hand and scurried down to the Raleigh Road to cheer the men. She was aghast. The emaciated soldiers wore stained, tattered uniforms and had no shoes for their feet. Their horses limped, pulling wagons laden with the wounded. Zoa Ann called it "the most pitiable sight I ever beheld."

In April 1865, after battles between Raleigh and Morrisville, Confederate general Joseph Wheeler retreated through Chapel Hill. *Courtesy Library of Congress.*

A few men from Wheeler's cavalry broke away from the column, riding up into the Hargraves' yard. They stole all the corn from the barn. Zoa Ann begged an officer to leave some for the household. "Madam, I wish we could, but our horses are starving," he explained, adding, "If we don't take it, Sherman's men, who are just behind us, will get every grain of it."

General Wheeler set up his command post on Franklin Street near the Chapel of the Cross. On Easter Sunday, April 16, 1865, rather than face the enemy, he retreated.

Back at the Hargrave plantation, rumors flew that William Tecumseh Sherman was looting houses as he advanced. The white cook, Betsy, gathered her prized possessions. She threw on her seven dresses, one on top of the other. Later, as she sat under a tree fanning herself, a "negro boy" ran in from the fields. "Yankees!" he hollered, "The Yankees are coming!" Betsy spotted a massive blue column inching along the Raleigh Road. Petrified of guns, she ran to her bedroom and hid under the feather mattress.

Several troopers rode their horses up into the yard and "began rummaging through the house without ceremony." As they climbed the stairs, their swords "rattled against the steps—clank, clank, clank." The men entered Betsy's room and lifted the mattress. She shuddered in fear. "Come here boys," chuckled one of the Federals, "here's the dying Confederacy!" The men proceeded to the next room. Plucking Zoa Ann's son from the crib, they ran their hands under the mattress. Luckily, the household silver had already been buried in the orchard, so the men mounted their horses and rode off. Zoa Ann breathed a sigh of relief. Her precious boy had come through unharmed.

On the morning of Easter Monday, Federal forces under General Smith Atkins rode into the village. This would have spelled disaster if not for the actions of UNC president Swain. Just days earlier in Raleigh, he helped secure assurances from General Sherman that the university and its library would be saved from pillage. Indeed, Atkins's troops set up guards at every campus building. For two and a half weeks, some five thousand Federal troops camped on "the sloping fields just north of town, from the Tenney Plantation [today's Tenney Circle] westward for about a mile." The officers and their horses took shelter in the campus buildings. Sherman joked that his officers had the "best educated cavalry horses in the Union army." Some of Atkins's men were troublemakers. They "went flying all over town, ransacking the houses and taking anything they found suited to their tastes and purpose." It was even worse in the surrounding countryside.

The Civil War was effectively over on April 26, 1865, when Confederate general Joseph E. Johnston surrendered fifteen miles away in Durham. The bloody conflict claimed about 620,000 lives, including at least 30 Chapel Hillians.

One veteran returning to the village was Jesse Hargrave's son Fred, then nineteen. He served briefly in the First Regiment, North Carolina Junior Reserves, which mainly performed guard duty across the state. Fred's mother had died during the war. In her will, she attempted to "equalize" the family estate among her three children. Since Fred had already inherited the plantation, she left Robert 640 acres encompassing today's Dubose mansion at Meadowmont. Mary received the house in the village and a pair of carriage horses, plus "negro woman Sue" and her two-year-old child.

Confederate defeat freed all the slaves, and this left the southern economy in tatters. The village of Chapel Hill was thrown into deep poverty. Having invested heavily in Confederate securities and bank stocks, the university was $100,000 in debt.

In the fall of 1865, Fred Hargrave was among just twenty-two men enrolling at UNC. The university stood on the brink of financial ruin.

Said to be the handsomest man in Orange County, Fred entertained UNC faculty wives at parties with his beautiful tenor voice. His spirited team of horses dashed his shiny carriage wherever he went. "Mr. Fred was a great sport," quipped former family slave Fannie McDade. "He lived ten days every week, with Sunday thrown in extra."

Radical Reconstruction infuriated Democratic conservatives. In 1868, North Carolina adopted a new constitution. The biracial Republican Party took over state government, spelling big changes for UNC. In 1869, former professor Solomon Pool was installed as president. He talked of enrolling Black students. Southern aristocrats were indignant, refusing to send their sons to the university. The Ku Klux Klan exerted its own influence, invading Chapel Hill to terrorize UNC faculty.

On February 1, 1871, with enrollment at a new low and funding practically nonexistent, the university closed its doors. Village businesses were ruined: dry-goods stores and drugstores; doctors' and lawyers' offices; boardinghouses; tailor, blacksmith, shoemaker and saddler shops; and livery stables. The "best families" abandoned the village. So did many professors.

By January 1873, the village and university buildings were in a "complete state of ruin and decay," reported the *Wilmington Journal*. Fences had fallen down. Once-busy streets had grown up with weeds and grass. Windowpanes were broken at every turn. A corner of the East Building's roof had been knocked off by a fallen tree during a storm, and the floors inside were littered with fallen plaster. The other campus buildings weren't much better.

That March, after joining a mercantile firm in Wilmington, Fred Hargrave sold his 905-acre plantation. The buyer was forty-year-old farmer and ex-Confederate William F. Strowd, who had settled in Chatham County in 1861. He got the plantation for $7,000—less than $8 an acre. Raleigh's *News & Observer* described William as "a plain, unassuming gentleman, who possesses that quiet determination to succeed." He was placing his bets on Chapel Hill.

DEVOTED TO THE CONSERVATIVE Democratic Party—at least for now—William F. Strowd was elected a delegate to the state's 1875 Constitutional Convention. It swung power back to the conservatives. UNC reopened under a new regime. In celebration, Chapel Hill firebrand Cornelia Spencer rang the campus bell for thirty minutes. Reconstruction was over. White supremacy had won.

Buoyed by these events, no doubt, William Strowd took advantage of the village's new promise of prosperity. He built a sawmill west of Chapel Hill, helping restore the university and the village. He also enlarged his plantation by eighty-eight acres north of today's East Franklin Street along Bolin Creek, where he owned another mill. In the winter, Chapel Hillians went ice-skating on his millpond.

Farm leader William F. Strowd. Serving in North Carolina's 1875 Constitutional Convention, he helped restore white supremacy in the state. Daily State Chronicle, *July 4, 1890.*

William prospered along with the village. In 1880, while co-owning a dry-goods and grocery store at Franklin and Columbia Streets, he grew tobacco "with gratifying results." The next year, he enlarged his plantation by another ninety-three acres near town.

In the spring of 1886, William could hardly contain his pride. His only child, Robert Lee Strowd—named after General Robert E. Lee—was married in Pittsboro to the "accomplished and fascinating" Fannie Headen. As a wedding gift, William deeded Robert a "one half undivided interest" in the 1,090-acre plantation.

William's loving generosity didn't end there. In 1888, he deeded Robert a separate 350-acre tract of prime farmland. It included today's University Place Mall, Binkley Baptist Church,

Enrolled at UNC from 1882 to 1884, Robert Lee Strowd was just twenty-two when his father set him up as a "planter." News & Observer, *October 5, 1897.*

Willow Terrace Condominiums, Brookwood Condominiums and Camelot Village. A few months later, though, Robert sold the property back to his father for $1,900 in cash. Robert and Fannie were planning a large home for their growing family. In 1890, they built an Italianate Revival house on

Robert and Fannie Strowd's home, built in 1890. Fashionable for its day, it stands in disrepair at 51 Davie Circle. *Courtesy of the State Archives of North Carolina.*

today's Davie Circle. With southern tongue in cheek, they named it "Plum Nelly," as it was *plumb* out of Chapel Hill and *nearly* to Durham. Robert and Fannie eventually had six children together: Frank, Wallace, Bruce, Mary Louise, Grace and Elizabeth.

The high ground of Robert Strowd's property would forever be known as "Strowd Hill."

ROBERT BEGAN HIS CAREER as a farmer, relying heavily on Black labor. He cultivated cotton, corn, fruit, thoroughbred Jersey cattle, pigs, chickens and likely tobacco, timber and other crops. Unfortunately, agricultural prices were low and credit rates for supplies were high. The Strowd men were leaders in the Farmers' Alliance of North Carolina, a secret society pushing for economic reform to help farmers. Although alliance members gained seats in the state legislature in 1890, crop prices continued to fall.

In this circa 1892 photo, ladies standing on Piney Prospect (the site of today's Gimghoul Castle) gaze east to "Strowd's lowgrounds" (today's Glen Lennox area). *Kemp Plummer Battle Photograph Album of the University of North Carolina #P0100, North Carolina Collection Photographic Archives, Wilson Library, University of North Carolina at Chapel Hill.*

In 1892, alliance leaders pinned their hopes on the new Populist Party, also called the People's Party. It sought to empower farmers, laborers and small businesses. In that year's election, Populists won six seats in the state legislature. But in 1893, as the party began making inroads, an economic depression gripped the nation. Agricultural prices fell even further.

Robert diversified. Putting his faith in Chapel Hill's university-fueled economy, he opened a general store on the north side of the main business block. At the time, Franklin Street was a narrow dirt road. Robert and his children "went to and from their home in carriages and buggies or on foot, often through mud that made travel extremely difficult."

Populists had a banner year in 1894. In an unlikely coalition with the Republican Party, they gained more seats in the state legislature. Robert's father, William F. Strowd, was elected to the U.S. House of Representatives as a Populist. Representing North Carolina's Fourth Congressional District, he "stood squarely and without flinching upon the principles inscribed upon the banner of the People's party," raved Raleigh's *News & Observer*. On the stump, he could really get a crowd going. He won reelection in 1896.

IN OCTOBER 1897, THE *News & Observer* ran a feature story about Robert Strowd's "splendid" farm. Fortunately, it painted a vivid picture. "On this estate is some three hundred acres of rich and reliable low lands, most of it already cleared and drained which produces luxuriant crops," the reporter gushed. "Much of the up lands is also cleared and in good state of cultivation." Nestled in a "five-acre grove" was the Strowd home, amid a "broad wooded area relieved here and there by fields and farms and traversed by picturesque and never failing creeks." Robert had recently refused "a sum away up in five figures" for the farm, adding, "I am anxious to sell it because I have more land than I can conveniently and profitably hold and cultivate." He was stretched thin.

By March 1898, Robert was serving as chairman of the People's Party Executive Committee of Orange County. He vowed that it would "stand squarely by the Populist organization." Meanwhile, he was preparing to join his father in Washington, D.C., and put 1,090 acres on the market at fifteen dollars an acre. But the plan fell apart. His father, a firm advocate of white-controlled government, failed to get nominated that fall. His political career was over.

AROUND THE TURN OF the century, the nation's economy bounced back. In April 1899, the *Caucasian* in Clinton, North Carolina, raved, "It takes but a glance to see the rapidity of Chapel Hill's progress." There were new houses, shops and campus buildings; a new electric light plant; a new hotel with electricity; and improved roads. That July, the Bank of Chapel Hill proudly opened its doors, the "only institution of the kind" in Orange County. Robert Strowd recommitted himself to the village. In 1900, he became a longtime stockholder in the bank. The next year, he purchased the building that housed his general store on East Franklin Street. Carrying all sorts of goods, including furniture, it made him one of the village's leading businessmen.

His undeveloped land generated cash as well. In 1907, he began leasing eighteen acres in today's Glendale area to the nascent Chapel Hill Country Club for golf, tennis and equestrian pursuits. The clubhouse, owned by geology professor Joseph Hyde Pratt, was located near today's Hill Street off Davie Circle. With a stunning view of the surrounding countryside, it burned around 1920.

On March 12, 1911, after suffering three strokes, Robert's father died. He was seventy-nine. His obituary in the *Caucasian* called him "one of the oldest inhabitants of Chapel Hill, and one of the most respected citizens of the community." His landholdings passed to his wife.

Two years later, Robert, with political ambitions of his own, retired from the mercantile business. He broke with his father's conservative politics. In 1916, as a "staunch Republican," Robert ran as the party's candidate for North Carolina Secretary of State. He lost to incumbent Democrat J. Bryan Grimes, a former classmate at UNC. But Robert would soon find other avenues to public service.

WHEN THE UNITED STATES declared war on Germany in April 1917, patriotic fervor swept Chapel Hill. As the nation geared up to defeat fascism in World War I, UNC's liberal arts curriculum was ditched and military preparation became priority number one. Drills were conducted on campus day and night.

Robert Strowd served as secretary of the local Exemption Board and aided various war charities. Ironically, while his sons were exempt from service, his family lost three women during the span of the conflict. His eighty-year-old mother died in February 1917. His wife of thirty-two years, Fannie, died in January 1918. Then, that October, his twenty-four-year-old daughter, Mary Louise, a Salem College graduate serving as chief clerk to the local Draft Board, died in the 1918 influenza pandemic. Robert's only consolation—if he had one—was inheriting his family's extensive landholdings. He now owned an estimated 1,400 acres just outside the village.

By the time of the armistice of November 11, 1918, some nine million men had made the casualty lists. Sadly, they included Chapel Hillians John Allen (Black), Willard A. Clark and Paul E. Sparrow.

AROUND 1919, ROBERT STROWD began a longtime role as vice-president of the Bank of Chapel Hill. As such, he helped many village businesses get off the ground. He probably helped many villagers buy their first homes, as well.

During peacetime, in July 1921, Robert began serving as postmaster of Chapel Hill. He resigned in March 1923, about the time he completed the two-story brick Strowd Building, longtime home to Sutton's Drug Store. He also played a major role in another local icon, serving on the Building Committee of today's University United Methodist Church. Meanwhile, he had a grand new vision for his farm: suburbs "in the manner of real cities."

Sutton's Drug Store was established in the Strowd Building in 1923. *Courtesy Allen Browne.*

By 1925, AMERICANS WERE enjoying unprecedented prosperity. It seemed the bull market would go on forever. Optimism soared. Robert's acreage in the eastern outskirts of Chapel Hill had skyrocketed in value. The automobile had become affordable to the common man, and an eighteen-foot-wide strip of concrete had been laid on today's East Franklin Street from the center of town to the Durham County line. UNC had garnered a national reputation, and the state was funding construction of a massive campus expansion. The growth of the university and the village seemed unstoppable. Incidentally, the new Gimghoul development was quickly filling up, so UNC professors and staff would soon be eyeing property just outside the town limits.

If Robert was waiting for precisely the right moment, this was it. Contacting his friends at the Chapel Hill Insurance and Realty Company, he put 1,200 acres up for sale. With reference to today's landmarks, the irregularly shaped tract was bound by the Willow Terrace Condominiums on the north; Rogerson Drive on the east; Raleigh Road on the south; and Battle Park, Carolina Avenue and Hidden Hills on the west.

The realty company capitalized on Lost Cause fervor, dubbing the Strowd farm the "Strowd Plantation." A March 1925 advertisement trumpeted: "The land is ideally sitinuated for a residential development. It is a fine place for a club; and the lower hills and the meadowland to the east would make a beautiful golf course." Unfortunately, the acreage didn't sell intact as hoped.

The two parties agreed to an alternative, if more convoluted, plan. The realty company would auction off parcels in the desirable, paved Durham Road corridor, roughly from today's Davie Circle to Bolin Creek. Then, it would purchase the rest of the 1,200 acres, netting Robert at least $125,000.

The auction was slated for April 22, 1925. To entice speculators, advertisements dangled a "long period" for payment: 10 percent cash down and the balance in nine equal annual installments. Buyers could customize their lot by purchasing three or more twenty-five-foot-wide parcels for homes or small farms. The gigantic land sale was the buzz of Chapel Hill.

A crowd of speculators gathered promptly at 10:30 that morning, despite the rain. The auctioneer announced that this would be a "first-class development—that lights, water, streets and sewers would be installed." In the frenzy of the moment, bids soared. When the hammer banged for the last time, thirty-one investors had claimed a total of about 100 acres, reaping approximately $78,000 (more than $1.3 million in 2022 money). Prime, wooded lots closest to town commanded about $1,900 per acre.

Strowd Plantation For Sale

1,200 Acres of Beautiful Hills and Meadowland, on the Edge of Chapel Hill and alongside the Paved Chapel Hill-to-Durham Boulevard, Are Put on the Market

Just outside of the eastern limits of the town of Chapel Hill is the tract of land known as the Strowd Plantation. It lies along both sides of the Chapel Hill-Durham concrete highway, running down the hill, and stretches southward to the Raleigh road.

The total area is about 1,200 acres. Most of it is high ground with splendid trees, but the easternmost part of about 300 acres, furthest from the town, down along the creek, is a level valley.

Before and for many years after the Civil War this land was the property of the Hargrave family. Jesse Hargrave bequeathed it to his children, Fred, Robert, and Mary. Mary married William Kenan. Her daughter, Mary Lily Kenan, became Mrs. Henry M. Flagler, and it was she who, a few years ago, gave to the University the fund of about two million dollars for the creation of the Kenan professorships.

Before the War the Hargraves, a wealthy family with many slaves, ran the place as a farm, and on it today there are seen walls and ditches that were built with slave labor. It remained in the possession of the family ten years after the war.

Fifty years ago, in 1875, it was bought by William F. Strowd of Chatham county, for many years one of North Carolina's Representatives in Congress. His son, Robert L. Strowd, came to live there upon his marriage in 1886 and it has been his home ever since. When his father bought it, the tract lay entirely south of the Durham road, but in recent years Mr. Strowd has added to it by purchases of land to the north of the road. On the estate are several dwellings, most of them new.

Like so much of the property in and around Chapel Hill, for a generation or more after the War the Strowd Plantation was valued only as farm land. People referred to it as a "country place." Mr. Strowd and his children went to and from their home in carriages and buggies or on foot, often through mud that made travel extremely difficult. But with the great growth of the University the town grew out to it, and, now that the concrete highway has been built, the owner motors from the bank or the post-office to his front door in about two minutes.

Within the last five years, he has received many offers, of from $3,000 to $4,000 an acre, for parts of the property adjoining the town limits. But Mr. Strowd has chosen to keep the place intact.

Now, at last, he has decided to put it on the market.

The land is ideally situated for a residential development, and of course it can be subdivided in any way the purchaser may elect. Streets and roads can be run through it, and every home that is built will be in easy reach of the University campus and the town. The slope of the land is such as to permit of a perfect drainage system.

It is a fine place for a club; and the lower hills and the meadowland to the east would make a beautiful golf course.

APPLY TO THE
Chapel Hill Insurance & Realty Company

To lend the Strowd farm an air of old South ambience, it was dubbed the "Strowd Plantation." Chapel Hill Weekly, *March 12, 1925.*

Among the winning bidders were Vernon Howell, charismatic banker and first dean of UNC's School of Pharmacy; Luther J. Phipps, manager of the Pickwick Theater and a future judge; and the entrepreneurial Jack Sparrow, who would soon open a filling station at the foot of Strowd Hill. Reportedly, a few speculators resold their lots "within a few minutes" at a "handsome profit."

Negotiations between Robert and the realty company continued for a day or two. As reported by the *Chapel Hill Weekly* on April 30, 1925, they shook hands on a grand total of $128,000 for all 1,200 acres (more than $2.1 million in 2022 terms). That meant the realty company got "the remainder of the farm, perhaps 1,100 acres, for just $50,000," the editor marveled. The Bank of Chapel Hill provided financing. Taking the lead as trustee was the bank's cashier, Milton E. Hogan Sr., one of Robert Strowd's closest friends.

Almost as soon as the auction was over, Robert began building a home on an oversized lot he reserved for himself at 741 East Franklin Street. He

In 1925, Robert Strowd built this handsome home at 741 East Franklin Street. It was the first house in Chapel Hill with central heat. *Photo by author.*

Left: Milton E. Hogan Sr., longtime cashier at the Bank of Chapel Hill. Locals saw him as an administrative genius and trusted ally. *Portrait Collection #P0002, North Carolina Collection Photographic Archives, Wilson Library, University of North Carolina at Chapel Hill.*

Below: Purchasing a lot at Strowd's first auction in 1925, pharmacist Carl Durham built a home for his family at 805 East Franklin Street. He became a U.S. congressman. *Photo by author.*

shared his newfound wealth. He gave each of his children $10,000 in cash (about $170,000 in 2022 terms). He also established a $5,000 scholarship in memory of his deceased daughter, Mary Louise, at her alma mater of Salem College.

IN JULY 1925, it seemed Chapel Hill might get another college—and on the former Strowd farm, no less. While Atlantic Christian College's president Howard Hilley was in the village, Mayor William Roberson offered him a choice of three twenty-five-acre sites, one of them on unsold Strowd property. Not coincidentally, Roberson was president of the Chapel Hill Insurance and Realty Company. He was anxious to spur land sales, but Hilley declined all offers.

That October, Chapel Hill Insurance and Realty changed its marketing strategy. It named a 1,500-acre tract after the famed William Richardson Davie, founding father of UNC. Combining the unsold Strowd acreage with other tracts along East Franklin Street, Davie Woods stretched from today's Davie Circle nearly to Booker Creek. Four hundred lots near the village would be auctioned on October 13, 1925. Davie and his cohorts had walked this very ground when searching for the university site, said an ad in the *Tar Heel*. "Coming from the east, they passed through virgin woods, stopping now and then to drink of the clear water of a spring, and to admire the trees and wild flowers," it added, claiming, "many of the very same trees, magnificent oaks and pines, under which these educational pioneers walked, are still standing."

The auction yielded twenty buyers, reported the *Weekly*, reaping about $52,000 (over $850,000 in 2022 money). Speculating on five lots on today's Davie Circle was nationally acclaimed engineer and architect Thomas C. Atwood. He was supervising the university's grand expansion project, including Kenan Stadium, Wilson Library and the Carolina Inn.

Another land sale of the period deserves mention. The Town of Chapel Hill purchased twelve acres of the Strowd farm on the south bank of Bolin Creek for its first advanced sewage treatment complex. Today, ironically, the site smells of sweet roses from a public rose garden.

In the fall of 1926, the Chapel Hill Insurance and Realty Company sold a sixty-one-acre tract of the Strowd farm bordering Raleigh Road. To the company's great disappointment, they got barely $100 an acre. Turns out, a mild recession had tanked real estate prices. Chapel Hill Insurance and Realty was doomed. In November 1927, the company declared bankruptcy.

Its court-appointed receivers, including Milton E. Hogan, were faced with liquidating holdings in and around Chapel Hill. That included a number of "brick store buildings" and "beautiful residences" in the village, plus all the unsold Strowd property—an estimated five hundred to six hundred acres. Holding a rash of auctions, the receivers managed to unload many properties without too much pain.

But the Strowd farm was another matter. An auction in May 1928 "revealed a degree of depression which surprised both sellers and buyers," commented the *Weekly*. Bids averaged a paltry thirty dollars an acre. Invoking their legal right to refuse sales, the receivers attempted to re-auction parcels on multiple occasions. But time wasn't on their side. "The Strowd farm affair is still in something of a tangle," the paper remarked that November. Of course, things went from bad to worse when the stock market crashed in the fall of 1929. Within a few short months, the receivers were forced to surrender the unsold Strowd farmland—some three hundred acres—to the Bank of Chapel Hill. Apparently, major investors in the realty company lost their shirts.

Pharmacist Philip Lloyd built this bungalow at 13 Davie Circle about 1929, when the street was called Strowd Place. *Photo by author.*

THE GREAT DEPRESSION HIT the village of Chapel Hill with a deafening crash. The state slashed UNC's budget, plunging the university into crisis. Professors' salaries were cut by one-third or more. Many businesses in the village were ruined. In November 1930, the *Daily Tar Heel* echoed the hopelessness of the era: "The word prosperity has slowly in the last year or so disappeared…probably never to return."

Like most area farmers, Luke Conner was in a world of hurt. In May 1929, he purchased 254 acres in "Strowd's lowgrounds" for a dairy farm. No sooner had he completed a ten-room house for his family than the Depression hit. If not for a friend's generosity, Conner would have faced swift foreclosure. To save the farm over the lean years, he sold off 60 acres of land. He also sold butter, eggs, hay and wood. The hickory was used to make Louisville Sluggers.

In mid-1932, Chapel Hillians heard an odd, shrill blast from the center of town. They traced it to a steam whistle at the Ford dealership, owned by Robert Strowd's son Bruce. "We wanted to let people know that times were beginning to get better, and so we decided to tell 'em with this whistle," Bruce enthused. "We blow it every time we sell a new car."

Luke Conner's dairy farm, circa 1955, with Strowd Hill in the background. On the site today are University Place Mall and Willow Terrace Condominiums. *Courtesy Laura May Conner.*

Banker Milton E. Hogan tested the waters, auctioning a fifteen-acre parcel of the Strowd farm in today's Glendale neighborhood. The news wasn't good. He barely got sixty-seven dollars an acre.

There was no shortage of hard-luck stories. C.H. Weaver lost his 375-acre dairy farm on today's Weaver Dairy Road, as well as a 25-acre estate at the foot of Strowd Hill. But one man's misfortune was another man's opportunity. In September 1932, UNC pharmacy professor Henry Burlage purchased the 25-acre property at auction for just sixty-four dollars an acre and moved his family into the existing home at today's 111 Meadowbrook Drive. Burlage was a serious gardener. While a Jersey cow grazed in his meadow, he grew apples, peaches, plums and raspberries. His wife, Alleda, grew prizewinning gladioli.

The Depression deepened. Many banks failed across the nation, triggering massive unemployment. On March 3, 1933, the eve of Franklin D. Roosevelt's inauguration, the United States was in a severe banking crisis. The next day, families gathered around radios for his inaugural address. "The only thing we have to fear is fear itself," he declared. Some Chapel Hillians might have begged to differ.

The new president moved swiftly to stabilize the economy and put Americans back to work. This was his New Deal. On Monday, March 6, he declared a "bank holiday." It suspended banking transactions nationwide for the entire week, halting the bank runs and allowing Congress time to enact banking reform laws.

Then, beginning in June 1933, bank deposits were insured by the federal government. This restored "sanity and confidence," said John B. Woosley, distinguished professor of economics at UNC. The following month, when Hogan auctioned a forty-two-acre parcel atop Strowd Hill, Woosley was the winning bidder. He got it for just sixty-seven dollars an acre. To supplement their meager Depression-era salaries, he and three fellow economics professors pooled their resources to develop Hillcrest. With land cheap and plentiful, they marked off lots ranging from one to five acres. One of the first buyers was Oliver K. Cornwell, who came to UNC in 1935 to modernize the physical education department. Another early resident was history professor Hugh Lefler, renowned for his books on North Carolina history.

Meanwhile, a stone's throw away at Robert Strowd's home, his health was failing. His eldest son, Frank, moved in and kept vigil. But in April 1934, just as Robert was nearing his end, Frank died of a stroke. Three weeks later, on May 7, Robert died at age seventy. According to his wishes, the family held a

This Dutch Colonial at 201 Hillcrest Road was completed in late 1933 by economics professor and World War I veteran Harry Wolf. He was an investor in Hillcrest. *Courtesy Whitcomb Rummel.*

Oliver K. Cornwell completed this stately Colonial Revival at 209 Hillcrest Road in 1940. He served as mayor from 1954 to 1961. *Photo by author.*

A surprising number of homes were built during the Depression, like this one at 9 Davie Circle. Labor and materials were cheaper. *Photo by author.*

private funeral in the home, followed by burial at Old Chapel Hill Cemetery. While the bulk of Robert's estate passed to his four surviving children, he left $1,000 to "trusty friend" Milton Hogan. That equates to about $22,000 in 2022 money.

The Bank of Chapel Hill's board of directors paid tribute to Robert for serving twenty-nine years as director and fifteen years as vice-president:

> *At all times he labored faithfully, zealously, and with genuine pride for the best interests of customers and stockholders, and was ever anxious to help in building up a strong bank to serve the town and surrounding country. This bank will miss his practical advice, his wise counsel, born of a successful business experience, and his punctual and helpful attendance at the weekly meetings of the board of directors. His interest, his constant thought for the*

welfare of the bank, and his valuable suggestions contributed largely to the present strength of the institution.

Although Robert Strowd has faded into obscurity, the town would be a very different place today if not for him. As a prominent banker, businessman, landholder and style-maker, he was important to the village's prosperity, growth and image.

PHARMACIST CARL DURHAM WAS one of the lucky ones. By mid-Depression, he had amassed about one hundred acres on Strowd Hill near his home. Joining the Orange County commissioners in 1932, he led the charge to extend electric lines to western Orange County farms—putting more than five hundred people back to work during the Depression. He became a long-serving U.S. congressman.

Investing in an even bigger chunk of the Strowd farm was local playwright and philosophy professor Paul Green. Despite the hard times, his career was on fire. He wrote screenplays for Hollywood films. By early 1934, he had amassed about 212 acres bordering Raleigh Road. After selling a parcel between Battle Park and Davie Circle, he built a home for his family. Then he began planning his Greenwood development.

Paul Green's home at 610 Greenwood Road. Here stood the plantation home of Jesse Hargrave. Shortly before Green's land purchases, this site was under consideration for a country club. *Photo by author.*

In 1939, wealthy artist William Meade Prince built this stately home at 707 Greenwood Road. He coined the phrase *The Southern Part of Heaven*. *Roland Giduz Photographic Collection #P0033, North Carolina Collection Photographic Archives, Louis Round Wilson Special Collections Library, University of North Carolina at Chapel Hill.*

Hard-charging developer "Joe Buck" Dawson built his Cape Cod home at 1203 Hillview Road about 1939. Later, he built Clearwater Lake for another development. *Photo by author.*

The Depression finally ended around 1939. But the air remained heavy. Concern was mounting about the war in Europe. Debate raged on the UNC campus over the pros and cons of U.S. involvement.

Encouraged by the economic upswing, realtor-developer "Joe Buck" Dawson purchased forty-three acres on Strowd Hill. He built a home for himself and his wife, Mamie, on Hillview Road, with a scenic view of the valley below. In 1940, he got his Hillview development off to a fast start. Speed was a theme in Dawson's life. He helped bring NASCAR racing to the area.

In 1940, "living legend" Sim Nathan scooped up an estimated thirty-two acres of the old Strowd farm. Located on the north side of East Franklin Street, the irregularly shaped tract stretched from the Bolin Creek Bridge to Elizabeth Street. A long-serving town health official and county coroner, "Doc" Nathan was also Chapel Hill's first veterinarian. His animal hospital was in a former roadhouse (now Vine's Veterinary). A "masterly man of the times," Nathan was a rotund 425 pounds. Within a few years, he had built a juke joint with carhops serving sandwiches and beer at 1215 East Franklin

This charming home at 3 Oakwood Drive was completed in 1942 while owned by the Fitch Lumber Company. Vegetation cleverly conceals a large addition. *Photo by author.*

Street. Named the Curve Inn (for the curve then in that stretch of road), it was "THE place for Chapel Hill's college and younger set."

In the interim, a prominent Chapel Hillian found a way to increase home ownership for UNC's service employees. Livingston B. Rogerson, business manager of the university, suggested that the employees form a housing cooperative. They jumped at the chance. Under the auspices of the Service Employees Corporation, they purchased forty-four acres of former Strowd land and assisted builders after hours in clearing, grading, plumbing, wiring, painting and more. By May 1941, the employees—including electrical engineer Grey Culbreth—had completed at least seven cottages in the new development of Oakwood.

Just east of Oakwood Drive was a narrow tract owned by Rogerson's partner in private practice, UNC accounting professor Erle E. Peacock Sr. He tasked Rogerson with developing the tract, giving rise to Rogerson Drive. A longtime resident was county employee Miss Woodward Byars, who taught domestic skills and home economics to women living in rural areas.

By September 1941, Henry Burlage had built a cottage or two on his twenty-five-acre farm. The Hidden Hills development was born. Happily, more ordinary Chapel Hillians were living the American dream.

CHAOS INTERVENED THAT DECEMBER, when Japan attacked Pearl Harbor. Young men and women of Chapel Hill left in droves to serve their country, including UNC faculty and staff. Development halted on the old Strowd farm. Indeed, the federal government brought all construction in the nation to a halt except for emergency purposes.

The Carolina campus was transformed into a military camp. There were seven different military training units, including a Naval Aviation Pre-Flight Training School. That first year, future president Gerald Ford was a platoon officer at the pre-flight school. He rented a one-room cabin from Henry Burlage in Hidden Hills.

Women did their part on the home front. Corielle Ellis of Davie Circle burned the midnight oil, sewing insignias on caps for the cadets. Oma Woosley of Hillcrest took nursing courses from the Red Cross in case of emergency during the shortage of trained nurses. Mrs. Alpha Wettach, who founded the Chapel Hill Experimental Kindergarten, collected scrap metal and sold war bonds. It was a time of gas rationing, Victory gardens and "Meatless Tuesdays."

Needless to say, World War II was a long-grinding death machine. There were a staggering fifty to eighty-five million casualties worldwide, including Chapel Hillians Bynum G. Crabtree, Lawrence Flinn, Carl C. Hogan, Whitney F. Poythress and John W. Umstead III.

On August 15, 1945, Franklin Street erupted with glee. Japan had surrendered, and the terrible war was over. UNC students screamed and danced while liquor flowed like water. A bonfire raged in the middle of the street. Confectioner Edward Danziger set a fifty-pound barrel of candy outside his store, and jubilant navy cadets tossed handfuls of the stuff into the air. Cars clogged the street with partygoers piled on top yelling cheerful greetings back and forth.

IN THE FALL OF 1946, another shock wave hit Chapel Hill. Nearly 4,500 veterans taking advantage of the GI Bill flooded UNC. Suddenly, the village had a severe housing shortage. Married students crammed into trailers, barracks and Quonset huts. Some students lived in tents.

In fact, returning veterans triggered a housing shortage nationwide. The federal government stepped in to help. New regulations promoted construction of moderate-priced housing, with veterans given priority as

Amid the student housing crisis after World War II, this rental home at 30 Davie Circle was built quickly with cinderblock. *Photo by author.*

buyers. Chapel Hill's Board of Aldermen created the Veterans' Housing Commission, which transported prefabricated, government-surplus houses from Portsmouth, Virginia, and rebuilt them for local veterans. Whichever housing option veterans chose, large swaths of the former Strowd farm stood ready to serve.

Cottages sprang up close to campus on Davie Circle, including one of the government's four-room "pre-fabs." Joe Buck Dawson, one of the village's "most active builders under the government-sponsored plan to provide houses for veterans," erected at least four prefabricated houses in his Hillview development. Henry Burlage built a few more cottages in his Hidden Hills development, which he enlarged to about forty-four acres during the war. Cottages also sprang up on Oakwood Drive, and in 1947, the Federal Housing Authority built thirty of them along Rogerson Drive. As quickly as builders hammered and sawed, however, they lost pace with demand. By the late 1940s, Chapel Hill was desperate for a solution.

In July 1949, it seemed the village had found its savior. He was area contractor William Muirhead. After discussing the housing shortage with acting UNC president William D. Carmichael Jr., Muirhead purchased forty-three acres of former Strowd land and broke ground on 314 one-level

Shown here is 102 Hoot Owl Lane in Hidden Hills. It was built about 1947 for Captain Donald W. Loomis, who served in both world wars. *Photo by author.*

Top: This 1948 home at 716 Greenwood Road belonged to Clifford Lyons, head of UNC's English department. Here, he hosted poet and friend Robert Frost. *Photo by author*.

Bottom: Built in the early 1950s, the award-winning Glen Lennox Apartments complex was planned by prolific Raleigh architect Leif Valand. He still had a few surprises for Chapel Hill. *Roland Giduz Photographic Collection #P0033, North Carolina Collection Photographic Archives, Louis Round Wilson Special Collections Library, University of North Carolina at Chapel Hill*.

apartments. Phase one of Glen Lennox was completed along Raleigh Road in June 1950. Among those flocking to the "picturesque colony" was "pretty Mrs. Ardith Johnson," secretary to UNC's new president, Gordon Gray. The next year, when President Harry Truman appointed Gray to head up the nation's psychological warfare unit against communism, Johnson pitched in. Another early Glen Lennox tenant was Milton Julian, who owned Milton's Clothing Cupboard on West Franklin Street.

ON AUGUST 1, 1950, the Town of Chapel Hill annexed 275 acres in the East Franklin Street corridor. Every bit of it was former Strowd property, including Davie Circle, Carolina Avenue, Roosevelt Drive, Hillview Road and Hillcrest. "Wherever you go in the suburbs you see home-building in progress," remarked the *Weekly*. "Local contractors are so busy that they cannot take any more work. The real estate agents are besieged by applications for houses both for rent and for sale."

By 1951, William Muirhead was planning another eighty apartments at Glen Lennox. The university was expanding its two-year School of Medicine into a four-year school and erecting the North Carolina Memorial Hospital. UNC was also establishing a new School of Dentistry and expanding the School of Nursing. All those newcomers would need decent, affordable housing.

Chapel Hill had another growing pain. Traffic congestion had long plagued Franklin Street in the center of the village. In the fall of 1950, after negotiations between state highway engineers and representatives of the university and town, construction began on today's 15-501 Bypass. Completed in 1953, the two-lane highway ran through former Strowd farmland, claiming slices of Greenwood, Oakwood and Luke Conner's dairy farm.

In 1952, William Muirhead completed Chapel Hill's first "modern" shopping center at Glen Lennox. Designed by Norwegian-born architect Leif Valand, it featured a Sinclair Gas station, the Colonial Grocery Store,

The Glen Lennox Shopping Center came on the scene in 1952. The Dairy Bar featured milkshakes, banana splits and other ice cream treats. *Roland Giduz Photographic Collection #P0033, North Carolina Collection Photographic Archives, Louis Round Wilson Special Collections Library, University of North Carolina at Chapel Hill.*

the Dairy Bar, a branch of the Bank of Chapel Hill, a laundromat and a post office. But not all citizens cheered. Chapel Hill, some said, was no longer a village. The *Weekly* editor tried to reassure them: "No place where bob-whites run around in people's yards [has] lost its village character."

BY 1956, LUKE CONNER'S dairy farm was in trouble. Again. He was being squeezed out by the corporate dairy conglomerates. With few options, he planned to convert his farm into a residential development, Conner Ridge, named after a low ridge then defining the tract. Now in his mid-sixties, it was time for Conner to retire anyway. Though wistful, he told the *Weekly*, "I feel it is right that I sell this land and just keep a few lots around our home." That included two acres for his son Frederick and family. Having served in World War II as a radio operator, Frederick returned to Chapel Hill to help save the family farm. By this point, though, he preferred the life of a postal clerk.

Conner's twenty dairy cows were named after movie stars. In this circa 1955 photo, they graze on the site of today's University Place Mall parking lot. *Courtesy Laura May Conner.*

Left: Hard-toiling dairy farmer Luke Conner, circa 1955. In his younger days, neighbors would see him "haying in the moonlight at midnight." *Courtesy Laura May Conner.*

Below: Luke Conner and grandchildren enjoy an idyllic summer's day at his pond around 1955. Today, Willow Drive runs through the site. *Courtesy Elizabeth Conner Jones.*

Luke Conner's son Frederick (*left*) and father in-law, Michael J. Boehm (*right*), in 1951. The dairy sold milk to Long Meadow Farms, a popular brand in Chapel Hill kitchens at the time. *Courtesy Elizabeth Conner Jones.*

Luke Conner partnered with leading Raleigh-based developer Ed Richards. It was a good match. In early 1956, Richards purchased twenty-nine acres of the Conner farm east of the bypass for a small housing development, Ridgefield.

IN JUNE 1956, THE town limits expanded again. More of Strowd's former property was annexed, including Oakwood, Greenwood and Glen Lennox. Ridgefield also made the list, even though home construction was only in the planning stages. Mayor Oliver K. Cornwell had recently said, "I don't think the Town can exist without spreading." Short of that, he warned, "the Town will be bankrupt in five years." Hidden Hills was annexed that July.

In the spring of 1957, new one-level homes went on sale in Ridgefield. One of the first buyers was Ward Peacock, a brilliant, up-and-coming executive at Erwin Mills in Durham. His wife, Barbara, a former beauty queen, had a degree in voice. The couple had a baby boy. Their next-door neighbors were the associate director of North Carolina Memorial Hospital, Gene Crawford; his wife, Virginia; and their twins. Ridgefield's baby-boomer families enjoyed outings to the Valley Drive-In Theatre on the bypass, which occasionally offered kiddie rides.

Development of the Conner dairy farm began in 1957 with Ridgefield ranchers like this one. They sold for just $9,900. *Photo by author.*

More locals joined the chorus saying that Chapel Hill's rapid growth had killed the village ambiance. Choosing his words carefully, the *Weekly* editor said Chapel Hill "has been fortunate in the extent to which it has kept its agreeable non-city-like atmosphere."

In fact, there were still over fifty undeveloped, wooded acres near the center of town. Former Strowd property, the tract bordered Battle Park. The Durham Realty and Insurance Company purchased the acreage from Marion Flinn (whose wealthy husband, Lawrence, was killed in World War II) and marked it off into fifty-seven ample lots for Glendale. Other developers had passed the property by because of the steep slope. The first homes were completed around 1959. Glendale was paradise to city planner Pearson Stewart, whose recipe for an ideal development required homes spaced to promote neighborliness and a natural buffer. Other early arrivals included professors "Mitch" Mitchell and his wife, Marlys Marie Mitchell. They eventually started up a local winery together.

In May 1959, a *Weekly* reporter put it bluntly. "Chapel Hill ain't a village any more, or even a town," he quipped. "Brother, we've got a city on our hands!" Not only was the university beginning another growth spurt, but the Research Triangle Park was also about to get off the ground.

In 1957, Luke Conner sold nearly five wooded acres for the Binkley Baptist Church. Soon, he forgave the note. "That's the kind of guy he was," remarked grandson Frederick Conner Jr.

The Willow Terrace Apartments (now Condominiums) were built in 1965–67 on the Conner dairy farm, coinciding with the northern border of the Strowd Plantation. *Photo by author.*

Top: 901 Willow Drive, built in 1967, housed the office of beloved pediatrician Bob Senior. Luke Conner's home stood just to the rear until about 1977. *Middle*: A modernist office building at 121 South Estes Drive, built on the former Conner farm in 1967. Designed by prolific local architect Don Stewart, it housed his architectural firm. *Bottom*: The Camelot Apartments, built in 1967 by veterinarian Lou L. Vine along South Estes Drive. Previously, he kept horses and goats on the property. *Photos by author.*

Luke inked his biggest land deal of all in October 1958, when developer Ed Richards purchased seventy-three acres west of the bypass. But Richards abandoned the idea of more housing. He had ambitious plans to build a $2.5 million strip shopping center. He consulted Raleigh architect Leif Valand, newly celebrated for his "modern" Cameron Village Shopping Center.

In Richards's high-stakes presentation to the town, he requested that the tract be rezoned for commercial use. Mayor Cornwell bristled, saying the project would undercut the planned Eastgate Shopping Center nearby. The Board of Aldermen rejected the rezoning request.

By 1964, it might have seemed that Richards would get his deal. The town had a new mayor, Sandy McClamroch, and the Board of Aldermen had rezoned the Conner farm for limited commercial use. Richards applied for a special-use permit. Again, he got turned down. Likely accustomed to such setbacks, he sold the acreage north of Willow Drive to realtor-developer Phil Rominger. An Ohio native and World War II veteran, Rominger built three bank branches, several low-rise office buildings and the Willow Terrace Apartments (now Condominiums). Meanwhile, Richards held out hope for his strip shopping center. Surely, before long, Chapel Hill's explosive growth would create enough demand.

5 Marilyn Lane, built in 1960. It was the award-winning home of architect Arthur Cogswell Jr., who left a legacy of midcentury modern residences throughout the area. *Photo by author.*

This modernist home at 104 Glendale Drive, designed by Arthur Cogswell Jr. and built in 1964, got a later addition by Louis Cherry. *Photo by author.*

This home at 333 Burlage Circle was built in Hidden Hills in 1964. The Craftsman-inspired dormer was probably added later. *Photo by author.*

Heavily influenced by Frank Lloyd Wright, Arthur Cogswell Jr. designed this 1966 home at 220 Glenhill Lane. *Photo by author*.

During Conner Ridge's development, construction was brisk in Chapel Hill's more established residential neighborhoods. Houses sprang up all across Robert Strowd's former lands, nearly fleshing out Hillcrest Circle, Davie Circle and the Greenwood, Glendale, Oakwood, Hillview and Hidden Hills developments. Scads of the homes were ranchers. Others were modernist, designed by celebrated local architects Don Stewart and Arthur Cogswell Jr.

IN THE EARLY TO mid-1960s, there was a flurry of construction along East Franklin Street. It gave rise to Masonic Lodge No. 408, the Bolin Meadow Apartments (now Village Green Condominiums) and Villa Tempesta, a "cultural center for the performing and fine arts" that eventually housed Whitehall Antiques. Just downhill from Dr. Vine's veterinary clinic, at 1217 East Franklin Street, he built a Colonial-style office building (first called the Professional Building) and Chapel Hill's first drive-through convenience

Masonic Lodge #408, right after construction in 1961 at 1211 East Franklin Street. Designed by Don Stewart, the modernist structure was considered at the height of vogue. *Roland Giduz Photographic Collection #P0033, North Carolina Collection Photographic Archives, Louis Round Wilson Special Collections Library, University of North Carolina at Chapel Hill.*

Designed by Kenneth Scott of Durham, this office building at 1407 East Franklin Street was built in 1963 for Collier Cobb & Associates. It was jokingly dubbed the "Collierseum." *Photo by author.*

store (now Sunrise Biscuit Kitchen). And, amid a call for good architecture, Collier Cobb & Associates built its stylish offices at the corner of East Franklin Street and Estes Drive (now an urgent care center). Undeveloped Strowd land was quickly dwindling.

IN AUGUST 1968, a decade after Ed Richards first petitioned the town for his strip shopping center, he had new drawings tucked under his arm. They revealed an "enclosed, air-conditioned" design by Leif Valand. Some Chapel Hillians lent their enthusiastic support, saying a modern mall would boost prosperity and, unlike the downtown business district, provide plenty of convenient parking. Others were rabidly opposed, arguing that a boxy mall and huge parking lot betrayed the town's charm and character. After protracted negotiations, the Board of Aldermen ended up split on the project. Howard Lee, Chapel Hill's first African American mayor, cast the tie-breaking vote to allow it. Earthmovers took a full year to elevate the construction site several feet to prevent flooding. University Mall finally opened its doors on August 2, 1973, with a ribbon-cutting by Lee and Richards. Richards's fifteen-year struggle was over.

Also in 1973, Brookwood Condominiums was built on South Estes Drive across from the mall. The buildings were designed by Arthur Cogswell Jr.

In 1979, the curtain opened on one last, slow-burning drama. Landworks Inc. got its hands on about twenty-four wooded acres from Carl Durham's heirs. Virtually the only undeveloped Strowd land left, it was near the top of Strowd Hill north of East Franklin Street. The town green-lit a low-density,

This 3,400-square-foot Franklin Hills home at 405 Deming Road was built in 1992. It was designed by Chapel Hill native John Bruce Hawkins. *Photo by author.*

Transitional home at 108 Hotelling Court in Franklin Hills, built in 1997. The street was named for Harold Hotelling, longtime professor in UNC's mathematical statistics department. *Photo by author.*

"environmentally-sensitive" condo complex, Franklin Hills. But in 1981, after just fourteen units were completed, there was an economic downturn—not to mention a glut of condo conversions in Chapel Hill. In 1985, local developer J.P. Goforth took charge, marking off the remaining acreage into fifty-two generous homesites. By the late 1980s, he had completed several distinguished single-family homes. Then, in the spring of 1990, plagued by financial, legal and health challenges, he took his own life. That wasn't the only disaster. The Great Recession began in 2007, followed by a full-on housing market crash in 2008. Development in Franklin Hills came to a screeching halt. Despite everything, though, the saga ended on a high note. With the completion of a seven-thousand-square-foot home around 2011, the neighborhood boasted a rich mix of architectural styles along rolling, curvilinear streets, with much of the forest intact.

AS WE'VE SEEN, IN the century since Robert Strowd sold his 1,200-acre farm, it was transformed beyond his wildest dreams. Due in large measure to today's mighty university, change seems incessant. The 15-501 Bypass has become a rush-hour logjam. More and more houses are demolished to make room for bigger, more contemporary ones. Every square inch of

Built in 2016, this large-scale, Craftsman-inspired home at 29 Oakwood Drive replaced a post–World War II cottage. *Photo by author.*

This home at 106 Carolina Avenue, built in 1971, has been completely modernized. *Photo by author.*

Happily, the town government reserved a sliver of former Strowd land for the Battle Branch Trail. It meanders through the woods from Forest Theatre to Valley Park. *Photo by author.*

Glen Lennox has begun a twenty-year redevelopment plan. The Gwendolyn Building (*at left*), completed in 2021, is named for Gwendolyn Harrison, the first African American woman to attend UNC. *Photo by author.*

land is coveted, as evidenced by sky-high real estate prices. A block of the time-honored Glen Lennox Apartments was wiped off the map for higher-density apartments and a four-story office building. And in 2021, the town approved a five-stage redevelopment of University Place Mall to include a seven-story apartment building.

So, hold on tight for the next century.

Professor Hedrick's Daring Stand
Against Slavery

Frémont is on the right side of the great question
which now disturbs the public peace.
—*UNC professor Benjamin Hedrick, October 4, 1856*

In the mid-1850s, when Benjamin Sherwood Hedrick became a professor at UNC, he seemed the consummate southern gentleman. But when he aired his mild antislavery views, he was labeled "a traitor and a scoundrel."

Born in 1827 in Davidson County, North Carolina, Hedrick was the son of a fairly prosperous farmer, bricklayer and slaveholder. In 1848, after attending Lexington Classical School in Salisbury, he entered UNC as a sophomore. He was a standout in mathematics.

After Hedrick's graduation in 1851 with "first honor in the senior class," UNC president David L. Swain recommended him for a position as clerk to the superintendent of the newly created U.S. Nautical Almanac Office in Cambridge, Massachusetts. It calculated positions of celestial bodies by which ships could navigate across the ocean. Hedrick began employment there in March 1851.

The North probably seemed an alien world to him. It was a hotbed of the antislavery movement and other social reforms. But Hedrick had an open mind, if not a sense of adventure. When he wasn't working or studying, he attended abolitionist sermons by famous preacher Henry Ward

Beecher and the fiery Thomas Parker. Hedrick was even a guest in Parker's home, describing the experience as "quite a treat." Hedrick's views were shifting due to osmosis, at the very least. But these weren't his only antislavery influences. His mother's side of the family had always opposed slavery.

Benjamin Sherwood Hedrick, 1857. *Benjamin Sherwood Hedrick Papers #0325, Southern Historical Collection, Wilson Library, University of North Carolina at Chapel Hill.*

IT WAS IN JANUARY 1854 that Hedrick returned to his alma mater, serving as its first professor of agricultural chemistry. It was a progressive program for its day. Students could receive full instruction in soil analysis and the use of fertilizers. Hoping to revitalize his native state's agriculture, Hedrick also edited the *Carolina Cultivator*, a periodical providing farmers with the latest practical information. He became a key figure in the state's agricultural reform movement.

At first, Hedrick and his wife, Mary Ellen, rented a small house. Then, on New Year's Day 1855, he purchased a three-acre lot at the intersection of Boundary and Franklin Streets for $300. He built a modest one-story house with a basement. The parlors were on the main level, and the kitchen and dining room were in the basement. In March 1855, Hedrick moved into his new home with his wife and their first of eight children. Before long, he added an "octagon-shaped study," which attracted many an eye in the village.

Professor Hedrick's troubles began in August 1856 while taking part in the election of state officials. After he voted for the slate of Democratic candidates, an acquaintance at the polls asked him whether he would vote the same ticket in the presidential election that November. Hedrick said he didn't know. Then he was asked if he would vote the Whig ticket. He said he would not. Lastly, he was asked if he would vote for John C. Frémont, the antislavery Republican candidate. He said he would—that is, if a Republican ticket was formed in North Carolina.

Hedrick's timing couldn't have been worse. During that bitter campaign season, the nation was more divided than ever on slavery. In recent years, slavery had become a vital part of North Carolina's economy, even in Chapel Hill. The Republican Party, on the other hand, was not only equated

Hedrick built the Horace Williams house's original portion (*center*) using cement and "rocks of various sizes." Eager to popularize this sturdy yet affordable construction method, he described the process in the *Carolina Cultivator*. *Photo by author.*

with robbing southerners of their rights and slave property, but also with encouraging slave insurrections and the consequent murder of southern whites. Word of Hedrick's declaration swept through the village like wildfire. Whites were indignant.

On September 13, 1856, a short editorial titled "Frémont in the South" appeared in Raleigh's *North Carolina Standard*, a leading Democratic newspaper in the state. "If there be Frémont men among us, let them be silenced or required to leave," asserted the writer. "The expression of black Republican opinions in our midst is incompatible with our honor and safety as a people." The paper's proslavery editor, William Woods Holden, was clearly targeting Hedrick.

Two weeks later, the *Standard* turned up the heat with an editorial written anonymously by UNC alumnus Joseph A. Engelhard. He wrote, in part:

> *We have been reliably informed that a professor in our State University is an open and avowed supporter of Frémont, and declares his willingness, nay, his desire, to support a black Republican ticket, and the want of a*

Frémont electoral ticket in North Carolina is the only barrier to this Southern professor from carrying out his patriotic wishes. Is he a fit or safe instructor for our young men?...[O]ught he not to be "required to leave," at least dismissed from a situation where his poisonous influence is so powerful, and his teachings so antagonist[ic] to the "honor and safety" of the University and the State?...We must have certain security, under existing relations of North with South, that at State Universities at least we will have no canker-worm preying at the very vitals of Southern institutions.

Bruised by character attacks and "erroneous allegations," Hedrick was in a quandary. Should he lie low, hoping the whole thing would blow over? Or should he explain his honorable motives? Against the advice of friends, he chose the latter. On October 4, 1856, he published his defense in the *Standard*. He claimed that he didn't support abolition; he simply opposed the expansion of slavery into the western territories. He reminded readers that revered patriots George Washington, Thomas Jefferson and Patrick Henry "were all opposed to slavery in the abstract, and were all opposed to admitting it into new territory." Hedrick asserted that Frémont had the mettle for the job, saying, "Platforms and principles are good enough in their places; but for the Presidential chair, the first requisite is a *man*." Hedrick also gave an economic argument. He contended that slavery had forced many non-slaveholders in the state to migrate westward in recent decades, "knowing, as they did, that free and slave labor could not both exist and prosper in the same community."

Hedrick's editorial backfired. During that chapter in southern history, anything less than full-throated support for slavery was considered heresy. Whites in the state lumped him in with the radical abolitionists. In Chapel Hill, UNC students burned him in effigy.

University officials were in a dither. The controversy could destroy the school's sterling reputation. On October 6, 1856, President Swain called a meeting of the entire faculty. After all thirteen were seated, Swain proclaimed:

In an institution sustained like this, by all denominations and parties, nothing should be permitted to be done calculated to disturb the harmonious intercourse of those who support and those who direct and govern it. And this is well known to have been the policy and practice during a long series of years.

After discussing the matter, a committee passed resolutions denouncing Hedrick's political views. The university could only prosper, they reasoned, if it avoided partisan politics.

Five days later, the matter was passed up the chain to the executive committee of UNC's Board of Trustees. They agreed that Hedrick had committed one of the university's cardinal sins by becoming "an agitator in the exciting politics of the day, which…injure[d] the prosperity and usefulness of the institution." They resolved that "Mr. Hedrick has greatly if not entirely destroyed his power to be of further benefit to the university in the office which he now fills." Translation: he was fired.

Hedrick believed he was treated unjustly. Exercising his right to free speech had cost him his livelihood. UNC never had a rule prohibiting professors from engaging in political conflicts, he insisted—at least not a written one. Besides, he never tried to convert a single student to his own views. He wrote: "The trustees have never been able to assign any reason for my dismissal, except that Holden and the mobocracy required it, and Holden and the mobocracy must be obeyed or the stars might fall, or some other equally great calamity happen to the state." Liberty meant nothing, Hedrick opined, if you couldn't "claim a voice in the election of a President."

BENJAMIN HEDRICK'S ORDEAL WASN'T over. On October 21, 1856, seventeen days after he published his defense, he attended an educational convention in Salisbury near his boyhood home. Held at the local Presbyterian church, it focused on reforming North Carolina's backward education system. Appointed a delegate weeks earlier, Hedrick hoped for a less hostile atmosphere in the western part of the state, which was historically more ambivalent toward slavery. He sat with his former professor Jesse Rankin. As Hedrick exited the church after the day's proceedings, dozens of outraged local citizens were there waiting for him. They promptly burned him in effigy. A sign attached to the flaming figure warned, "Leave or [face] tar and feathers." Hedrick fled to Rankin's home. Just after he entered the house, the crowd came up. Hissing, shouting and clanging cowbells and tin pans, they threatened to burst into the house after him. Luckily, a few prominent citizens showed up and dispersed the mob. Hedrick escaped by freight train to his brother's house in Lexington, eventually making his way back to Chapel Hill.

But the village was a dangerous place for him. The editor of Raleigh's *Standard* fumed, "No man who is avowedly for John C. Fremont for President, ought to be allowed to breathe the air or to tread the soil of North Carolina." The situation was hopeless, Hedrick told his wife, since "those who are against me are perfectly mad." With no time to spare, he packed up, sold his Franklin Street home and fled north with his family.

If there were other would-be dissenters in Chapel Hill, they had learned to keep their mouths shut.

3

GREENWOOD, ACT I

A Tight-Knit Collective of Artists

*Mr. and Mrs. Paul Green, on their way home from
California in two automobiles, are expected to arrive today.*
—Chapel Hill Weekly, *July 7, 1933*

During the Great Depression, many Chapel Hillians were strapped, or worse. But not philosophy professor, playwright and poet Paul Green. He got a lucrative gig. In February 1932, he eagerly headed off to Hollywood with a contract to write a screenplay for Warner Bros. Laboring for weeks on a script for *The Cabin in the Cotton* starring Bette Davis, he agreed to a few minor revisions. But when he saw the final film, his heart sank. His carefully crafted script had been dumbed down for the masses. Another writer explained, "Listen, this is a business out here, not an art." Though Green was disillusioned, he had hope for cinema as an art form. He urged producers to raise their standards.

Green merited more Hollywood contracts. By early 1933, he had written screenplays for *Voltaire* starring British actor George Arliss and two films showcasing Will Rogers, *State Fair* and *Doctor Bull*.

In the summer of 1933, Green returned to Chapel Hill with his savings. Local banker Milton E. Hogan urged him to invest in land east of town. Chapel Hill was growing in that direction, and real estate was selling at half of pre-Depression prices. But Hogan had his own motives. As receiver for the bankrupt Chapel Hill Insurance and Realty Company, he needed to unload vast swaths of land for the bank.

Reluctant at first, Green decided to jump in. An avid naturalist, he longed for the soulful expanse of green fields and meadows like those of his youth on a cotton farm in Harnett County. He once wrote, "By forced laboring in the fields, association with plants, animals and birds and long experience with wind and weather, I gradually grew to love the earth and sky for themselves alone."

By early 1934, he had amassed about 212 acres of meadowland and rolling forest encompassing today's Greenwood and surroundings. He paid just twenty-four to forty dollars per acre. He and his wife, Elizabeth Lay Green, had become enamored with the property about fifteen years earlier while students at UNC. During an "afternoon ramble," they arrived at a promontory with a sweeping view of countryside to the steeples of Durham. Once resting on the site was the Hargrave plantation house, its canopy of fine elms still standing.

Reserving eight and a half acres for his own small farm, Green wasted no time planting corn. As a base of farm operations, in 1934, he began building a small cottage on the plantation house site. He also put in a gravel drive connecting to Raleigh Road. To make it passable by automobile, he stood on the old road grader hooked to his tin lizzie while his ten-year-old son drove the car very slowly.

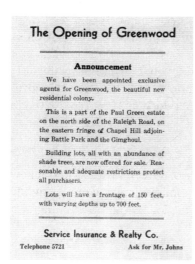

The Opening of Greenwood

Announcement

We have been appointed exclusive agents for Greenwood, the beautiful new residential colony.

This is a part of the Paul Green estate on the north side of the Raleigh Road, on the eastern fringe of Chapel Hill adjoining Battle Park and the Gimghoul.

Building lots, all with an abundance of shade trees, are now offered for sale. Reasonable and adequate restrictions protect all purchasers.

Lots will have a frontage of 150 feet, with varying depths up to 700 feet.

Service Insurance & Realty Co.

Telephone 5721   Ask for Mr. Johns

In June 1938, Green contracted with Service Insurance & Realty Co. to sell about one hundred acres of land for Greenwood. The name was coined by Louis Graves, editor of the *Weekly*. *Chapel Hill Weekly, June 10, 1938.*

Just east of Green's small farm was an old cemetery dating to the late 1700s. Researchers believe that slaves of the Barbee and Hargrave families are buried there. Green deeded the cemetery to the Town of Chapel Hill for safekeeping.

In early 1935, as he neared completion on his second novel, *This Body the Earth*, Green finished his cottage. It boasted a cozy, pine-paneled study—the perfect refuge for writing.

In 1936, after adding two wings to the cottage, he moved there with his wife, son and three daughters. Explaining the move to "the country," he quipped, "I don't want my boy to grow up without knowing anything about cows."

Green reveled in the natural wonders. The forest floor was sprinkled with native flowers like bloodroot and anemone. He identified seventy-one different kinds of trees. Compared to his former home at The Glen, the lay of the land unlocked brilliant, crimson sunsets. And the mineral spring below his house provided his favorite drink in the whole world.

The Green family's two-acre vegetable garden was plowed by a little brown pony. They also had chickens. And providing milk was their fine, purebred Jersey cow, Right Royal Double Louise.

BY THIS POINT IN his career, Green was determined to escape "the narrow confines of the usual Broadway play and stage." They simply couldn't convey "the richness of our tradition, folkways, singing, dancing and poetry," he explained. So he changed the rules. He created a new theater genre that he called "symphonic drama." It wowed audiences. Inspired by historical events—and set at or near the site depicted in the story—these under-the-stars spectacles were a fusion of dialogue, poetry, song, music, dance, pantomime and light. In the summer of 1937, Green staged his first such production, *The Lost Colony*, in Manteo, North Carolina. It told the tragic story of the famous sixteenth-century English colony that vanished without a trace. Among those praising the spectacle was Eleanor Roosevelt, "not only because of its historical interest," she said, "but because of its intrinsic beauty." *The Lost Colony* is Green's most famous work. It's been staged in Manteo every summer since, except during World War II and in 2020 due to the COVID-19 pandemic.

AFTER THE DEPRESSION LIFTED in 1939, many of Green's friends and fellow artists followed him to Greenwood Road, establishing a vibrant, tightly woven community. What follows is an introduction to that fascinating cast of characters.

NOEL HOUSTON (1909–1958)

Noel Houston was a critically acclaimed playwright and novelist. Coming to Chapel Hill in 1937 to study playwriting under Frederick Koch and Paul Green, he quickly blossomed. His stirring folk plays included *According to Law*, which center on a Black man framed for raping a white woman. In

1940, it ran for thirty-eight performances at the Provincetown Theater in New York.

Thanks to Green's influence, Houston was awarded Rockefeller Fellowships in playwriting for 1938–39 and 1939–40 and, in 1941, a Dramatists Guild Fellowship. "Eternally indebted," he said, he named his son Paul Green.

In 1941, Noel Houston and his wife, Kay, moved into a new home at 801 Greenwood Road. The neighborhood's Houston Road was named after him.

In the madness of World War II, he wrote a touching radio play about a young man killed in the war, *One Ted Malloy*. It was produced by UNC's Department of Radio for its *Men in Action* series, which focused on the founding and growth of American freedom. The series adapted stage plays by Paul Green, Elizabeth Lay Green, Earl Wynn and others. With Paul Green volunteering as literary consultant, the local programs quickly went national with the Mutual Broadcasting System.

Houston was known for his versatility. In 1941, he published *The Great Promise*, a bestselling novel in England. In the last year of his life, he was a popular lecturer at UNC.

JAN PHILIP SCHINHAN (1887–1975)

Born in Vienna and a graduate of the Church Music School at Regensburg, Bavaria, Jan Schinhan was a gifted musician, composer and conductor.

In 1935, after serving as head of the organ department at the San Francisco Conservatory, he came to UNC as a music professor. He taught organ, piano, composition and graduate courses in folk music. He composed over one hundred songs and anthems and served as director of the Institute of Folk Music. In 1939, he arranged organ music for Paul Green's latest symphonic drama, *The Highland Call*.

In 1941, Schinhan and his first wife, Camilla Jessie von Egloffstein Schinhan, built a Cape Cod home on four acres at 700 Greenwood Road. Camilla was an accomplished singer. Known in the village for her dramatic readings, she died in the Greenwood home in 1947.

Schinhan's second wife, Elizabeth Logan Schinhan, was a music instructor in Chapel Hill's public schools. With a strong background in voice, she sang solos with the UNC Symphony Orchestra.

JAMES STERLING TIPPETT (1885–1958)

With farm-boy roots, James Tippett was an educator and children's book author.

Landing in Chapel Hill in 1939, he and his wife, Martha, built a home the following year at 704 Greenwood Road. He clung to those six beautiful acres for the rest of his life.

In high demand as an educator, Tippett wrote every chance he got. Attempting to re-create his "everyday world of childhood," his stories feature gardens, machines, dogs and children, all of which fascinated him. His many children's books include *I Know Some Little Animals* (1941) and *Here and There with Henry* (1944), both featuring the adorable creatures of Greenwood. His best-known work is "Sunning," a poem about a dog sleeping in the summer sun that became required reading in many elementary schools.

The door to Tippett's study was always open to the neighborhood children. One woman recalled: "If there was a butterfly or insect collection to be organized, if a child had captured a rare species from the world of nature, or if some poem or idea needed encouragement or nourishment, Mr. Tippett…would stop his work and spend the time of day in the children's world. Ideas, books, and paper and pencil would come from the study, and much laughter."

WILLIAM MEADE PRINCE (1893–1951)

Raised in Chapel Hill, William Meade Prince was a gifted artist and memoirist.

After studying in New York from 1913 to 1915, Prince produced illustrations that appeared on the covers of national magazines like *Collier's*, *The Saturday Evening Post* and *The Country Gentleman*. They made him one of the best-known illustrators in America. His work could easily have been mistaken for that of Norman Rockwell.

Returning to Chapel Hill a wealthy man in the 1930s, Prince became a lecturer in UNC's Department of Art. In 1939, he and his wife, Lillian, built a stately brick Colonial Revival home on a double lot at 707 Greenwood Road.

Heading UNC's art department during World War II, Prince produced posters to aid the war effort. Many featured his portraits of wounded soldiers and sailors.

He even acted in several plays by the Carolina Playmakers. He played Ananias Dare in *The Lost Colony*, in which Lillian played the role of Queen

Elizabeth. Trained in New York, she acted in over thirty Playmakers productions.

William Meade Prince coined the phrase *The Southern Part of Heaven* as the title for his boyhood memoir. On November 10, 1951, at the age of fifty-eight, he shot himself in the studio of his Greenwood Road home. On Lillian's death in 1962, she left over $130,000 to the Playmakers.

ARTHUR PALMER HUDSON (1892–1978)

Growing up on a farm in Mississippi, Hudson came to UNC in 1930, where he served as an English professor for twenty-three years. He taught classes in folklore and helped lead the folklore curriculum. Folklore was his lifelong passion, much as it was Paul Green's.

In 1941, Hudson and his wife, Grace, built a home at 710 Greenwood Road. In his free time, he enjoyed writing simple poems. They were widely used in readers, language books, music books, anthologies and teachers' guides.

On the evening of March 3, 1961, while poet Robert Frost was in town for his thirteenth annual visit to UNC, the Hudsons feted him at a "conversation party" in their home. Guests included Professor and Mrs. Clifford P. Lyons, Chancellor and Mrs. William B. Aycock and the Greens. Hudson got the party started. Cognizant of Frost's phenomenal memory, he asked him to recite Samuel Taylor Coleridge's poem "Cologne." It describes the "stenches and stinks" of that famous German city. The crowd roared.

Hudson's major publications include *Folksongs of Mississippi and Their Background* (1936) and *Folklore in American Literature* (1958). He also wrote the folklore section of the *Literary History of the United States* (1948).

LYNN GAULT (1912–1998)

Mr. Lynn Gault first came under Paul Green's spell in 1937, when he arrived at UNC for graduate work with the Playmakers. Three years later, he joined the staff as stage designer.

Early in World War II, Gault was stationed near Los Angeles. Paul Green was in the city working on a Hollywood screenplay, and the two shared a warm reunion. Then, on the eve of Gault's deployment to the Pacific, he wrote his friend back in Chapel Hill, expressing his sincere hope of living in Greenwood after the war. Green wrote back, vowing to reserve a lot for him.

In December 1945, according to plan, Lynn Gault and his wife, Lucille, purchased a three-and-a-half-acre double lot. They built a home at 703 Greenwood Road (since demolished).

Picking up where he left off with the Playmakers, Gault created sets for productions like George Bernard Shaw's *Caesar and Cleopatra* and Jean Giraudoux's *Madwoman of Chaillot*. He was called "by far the busiest Playmaker of all" in 1950, when he became the first stage director for *Unto These Hills*, Kermit Hunter's symphonic drama staged in Cherokee, North Carolina. In the process, he became fascinated with ceramics. In 1952, he moved to the North Carolina mountains, purchased a potter's wheel, built an outdoor kiln and went into business.

In 1960, the Playmakers convinced him to return for the school year. His projects included creating sets for Richard Rodgers's enduring musical *South Pacific*.

EARL R. WYNN (1911–1986)

Earl Wynn arrived in Chapel Hill in 1938 as instructor of speech at UNC's Department of Dramatic Art. Organizing courses in radio acting and production, he produced and directed the *Men in Action* radio series. Occasionally, he played the role of Governor White in *The Lost Colony*.

In October 1941, Wynn and his first wife, Irene, purchased a lot on Greenwood Road. Just weeks later, Japan bombed Pearl Harbor. Wynn put his skills to work for the war effort, producing films as a civilian for the army and writing scripts in Hollywood for naval training films.

After the war, he became director of UNC's newly established Communications Center, which centralized the production of audiovisual media on campus. It broadened educational programming in the state.

In 1947, at Wynn's urging, the university created the Department of Radio. When it expanded to include television and motion pictures in 1954, he served as chairman. The next year, he took WUNC-TV Channel 4 on the air with educational programming.

In 1950, Wynn built a "California-style" home at the corner of Greenwood and Stagecoach Roads.

His second wife, Rhoda, earned a master's degree from UNC's drama department and became assistant professor in the Department of Radio, Television and Motion Pictures. Serving as Paul Green's assistant for fifteen years, she worked on his manuscripts. "He thought there was a place in theater for heroes, courage and high principles," she once said. "Most of his plays celebrate the courage of someone."

NATURALLY, GREENWOOD ALSO ATTRACTED Green's academic friends at UNC. They included William Poteat, a popular philosophy professor; and Clifford Lyons, head of the English department and a celebrated Shakespeare scholar.

In 1939, Green purchased an old log cabin from a widow near Hillsborough. He moved the sixteen-by-eighteen-foot structure, "log by log," down the hill behind his house. Rebuilding it himself, he added a stone fireplace and chimney. In the mortar of the structure's base, he inscribed a quote from Chaucer's prologue to "The Reeve's Tale." An entry from Green's diary on June 16, 1939, reads: "First day's work in cabin. Wonderful quiet." It's been said that the cabin "served as a retreat and source of literary inspiration to Green, who used the solitude and rustic ambience to tap his literary creativity." Indeed, he wrote in that cabin for twenty-six years.

Green moved his old, "wheezy" pump organ into the cabin. "Pumping potently with both feet and pecking out tunes with one finger," he arranged music for his 1939 symphonic drama *The Highland Call*.

Paul Green's son, a budding electrical engineer, secretly rigged a system of wires from his bedroom to the cabin. It was a crude intercom system. One day, while Green was in the cabin working away, a disembodied voice said, "Lunch is ready." Green jumped out of his skin, as if hissed at by a copperhead.

IN THE EARLY 1940s, during World War II, Paul Green gave Hollywood another chance. He wrote screenplays for Metro-Goldwyn-Mayer. But this time, he wasn't just disillusioned, he was disgusted. The "moneymakers" used cheap tricks, he said, rather than tapping the medium's "infinite" power for good. In a speech, he once said, "The men who control the movies are menaces to civilization."

Green was far happier writing folk plays, often centering them on oppressed Blacks. He hoped to open minds so that Black people weren't constantly pushed to the bottom. "We've had three hundred years of Negro talent, great voices, possible mighty singers, mighty poets, doctors, all gone to oblivion," he groaned. This cry for social justice inspired his 1927 Pulitzer Prize–winning play *In Abraham's Bosom*. He wrote other works to change attitudes about capital punishment. When it came to social issues, Green didn't tiptoe with politicians or anyone else. There are times, he said, "you have to use a red-hot iron on evil and burn it out."

A true rarity for Jim Crow America, Greenwood's written covenants didn't forbid Black residents. Green's early support for racial justice raised many an eyebrow, even in "liberal" Chapel Hill. His wife was stunned that he spoke out "more strongly than anyone else in the state" on the issue. In the summer of 1940, the *Weekly* reported that he was collaborating with "Negro writer, Richard Wright," adapting Wright's celebrated novel *Native Son* for the Broadway stage. As Green's biographer put it, "Paul Green was all set to sock damnable Jim Crow right in the snout." His wife expected to wake up one night and find a cross burning on the front lawn. It never happened.

IN EARLY 1943, AS Paul Green began writing the screenplay for *Captain Eddie* starring Fred MacMurray, he purchased sixty acres just north of Greenwood. In the lowlands near Bolin Creek, he created a two-acre lake for swimming and fishing.

While it's true that Green's Hollywood work afforded him land, it was the land itself that provided his family's financial security. Most of his writing paid poorly, and he really had to hustle to get it.

In 1944, Green retired from UNC to focus his energies on writing. "I can think of no better future for me than…the job of pounding a typewriter," he wrote from California to a friend in Greenwood. "I am irrevocably bitten by the writing bug." His last line waxed poetic: "I can visualize you folks there, the road, the green trees and the hot quiet summer afternoons with the far off dreamy call of the yellow-billed cuckoo, and the strident cry of the flicker high in some dead pine, and I know homesickness again."

Between trips to Hollywood and New York, Green cherished his days back home. As his lively imaginings poured forth onto paper, Chapel Hill mushroomed. In the early 1950s, the 15-501 Bypass cut along Greenwood's eastern border. Boat-sized cars whizzed by, spewing their noxious fumes. Around 1960, the Conner dairy farm just north of Greenwood was plowed under, and it seemed Green was about to get a commanding view of a massive strip shopping center. He sold a fourteen-acre tract near today's South Estes Drive, including his legendary log cabin study.

Then, in 1965, about the time he bid goodbye to Hollywood forever, he did the same to Greenwood. Selling his home with four acres, he moved to an old farmhouse in the country on Old Lystra Road, southeast of Chapel

Paul and Elizabeth Green at home in Greenwood, around the early 1950s. *Used by permission of the Paul Green Foundation.*

Hill. He called his farm Windy Oaks. Back in his element, he wrote as prolifically as ever. By the late 1970s, he'd created two novels, six volumes of short stories, five volumes of essays, sixteen symphonic dramas and more than a dozen Hollywood film scripts. He needed his assistant, Rhoda Wynn, just to keep track of it all.

Above: Paul Green's cabin, now nestled at its third home, the North Carolina Botanical Garden. *Photo by author.*

Left: Rhoda Wynn served as Paul Green's administrative assistant for fifteen years. In the 1990s, she helped save his cabin study. *Portrait Collection #P0002, North Carolina Collection Photographic Archives, Wilson Library, University of North Carolina at Chapel Hill.*

On May 4, 1981, while taking a nap at home, the brilliant and spirited Paul Green quietly slipped away. He was eighty-seven years old. A reporter sought Earl Wynn for comment. "Paul Green was the greatest human being I ever knew," he said. "In matters of human rights, he was far ahead of his time. He was always on the side of angels."

By 1991, PAUL GREEN'S cabin in Greenwood had fallen into disrepair. A group of concerned citizens, including Rhoda Wynn, launched a rescue effort. The North Carolina Botanical Garden graciously accepted the cabin. It was loaded onto a flatbed truck and hauled to the garden, where it was lovingly restored and renovated.

Today, the cabin is a permanent symbol of Paul Green's fascination with nature, botany and folk culture. It also provides a door into the world of a cutting-edge dramatist and humanitarian. So, by all means, step on in.

4

Mrs. Harold Walters Empowers '50s-Era Women

We're flooded with advice as to what
women should do, most of it contradictory.
—Adelaide Walters

In April 1957, fifty-year-old Adelaide Walters entered the race for a seat on Chapel Hill's Board of Aldermen. Until then, the board's conference table was exclusively a man's realm. But if anyone didn't take her seriously, they had two feet cemented in the past.

Born Adelaide Harvey in Upstate New York, Walters was no June Cleaver. A member of Phi Beta Kappa with a bachelor's and master's in history and government, she was a proven leader in civic affairs and grassroots organizing. She couldn't have done it with a typically sexist 1950s husband. She said hers was "most cooperative and willing to have me engage in activities outside the home."

An eighteen-year resident of Chapel Hill, Adelaide had no children. Determined to engage women voters and create a more perfect democracy, she served as president of the Chapel Hill League of Women Voters from 1950 to 1951. She was state president of the league from 1954 to 1956.

Adelaide was a founder and leader of Chapel Hill's liberal Community Church, which espoused "charity in all things." She lived her creed. She served as co-chairman of a clothing drive to benefit refugees of the Hungarian Revolution of 1956. As she entered the aldermanic race, she was vice-president of the North Carolina Council of Women's Organizations. Encouraging '50s-era women to break free of their apron strings, she taught

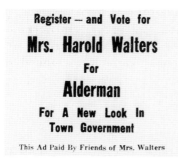

Register — and Vote for

Mrs. Harold Walters

For

Alderman

For A New Look In
Town Government

This Ad Paid By Friends of Mrs. Walters

In her campaign ads, Adelaide Walters went by the more formal title Mrs. Harold Walters. It probably rang better with male voters of the time. Chapel Hill Weekly, *April 19, 1957.*

them how to assume leadership roles. Surely, her work empowering women made her a darling of female voters.

Vivacious and poised with an easy wit, Adelaide said her background gave her "an intimate acquaintance with such basic matters as taxes, city budgets, subdivision regulations, and the uses and practices of the city-manager form of government." She also assured voters she understood the town's most pressing need: "The preservation of the unique charm and personality of Chapel Hill" during this period of explosive growth. The previous year, her neighborhood of Greenwood was annexed by the town, along with Glen Lennox, Ridgefield, Oakwood, Estes Hills, Hidden Hills and the Glenwood School area. In 1953, a new bypass stretched from one end of Chapel Hill to the other. The town's population had nearly doubled since 1950.

THE MUNICIPAL ELECTIONS FINALLY rolled around on May 7, 1957. Voters were to elect four aldermen from among seven candidates. When the votes were tallied, Adelaide defeated four of the male candidates to win a four-year term—a stunning result in the South for its day. Incumbents Hubert Robinson Sr. (the only Black alderman) and Paul Wager were reelected to another four-year term. Newspaperman Roland Giduz won a two-year term. Voters also approved a $500,000 bond issue, funding sewer lines and curbs and gutters in the newly annexed neighborhoods, plus a new fire station at Glen Lennox.

Sworn in six days later, Adelaide hit the ground running. Countless municipal issues had to be juggled on a tight budget, from street improvements and parking ordinances to personnel management and rezoning for development. She proved that women could be strong, forward-thinking leaders in government.

BACK THEN, THE ALDERMEN met in the brick, Federal-style Town Hall at the southwest corner of Rosemary and Columbia Streets. Citizens were invited to attend and voice their concerns. Adelaide welcomed public engagement, even if it meant complaints. "And why not?," she shrugged. "The demand for better schools, better recreation facilities, more governmental services are healthy signs of democracy at work. Political participation is not limited to a small group but extends to all segments of our community—even women and Negroes."

Between late 1957 and early 1958, there were "a number of minor conflicts between white and Negro teenagers" in the village. Adelaide took action. When the Board of Aldermen met in March 1958, she moved for the establishment of a biracial citizens' committee, called the Human Relations Committee. Seconded by Alderman Robinson, the motion passed unanimously. The committee's purpose was to encourage understanding and goodwill among all races, to promote the general welfare of the community and to act as a public forum in hearing complaints involving racial tension. Mayor Cornwell appointed a seven-member committee comprising Black and white townspeople. Organized that September, it would conduct intensive negotiations during the desegregation movement.

Adelaide helped establish Chapel Hill's first public library. In June 1958, the Board of Aldermen considered a request for a $4,600 appropriation for that purpose. Adelaide voted in favor with the majority. That December, a public library was set up in the first floor of an old clapboard house near Franklin and Columbia Streets. Some old-timers still remember it.

Apart from her work on the Board of Aldermen, Adelaide maintained a dizzying schedule of community service. In 1958, she served as co-chairman of the Community Chest campaign, which allocated funds to local service agencies. She taught Sunday school at the Community Church. She was a member of the Research Triangle Regional Planning Commission, which focused on "orderly" economic development in the counties surrounding the newly established Research Triangle Park. And she served on the town's Recreation Commission, which sought to establish parks and recreation programs for "both white and Negro youngsters." She asserted, "If we are interested in the future of our community, we must work for the welfare of our young people." The Recreation Commission led a three-year community-wide effort, culminating in Chapel Hill's first public park, Umstead Park. At first, in keeping with the times, it was whites-only.

Adelaide fought segregation. When local Black high school students launched protests in February 1960, many merchants believed they'd go broke if they served Blacks. Adelaide tried to calm fears. She signed a petition pledging "moral support and patronage to all merchants who will provide equal service to all their customers irrespective of race." Yet just as it seemed the civil rights movement had stormed into Chapel Hill, the demonstrations fizzled.

The town's first female alderman, Adelaide Walters, was a liberal among liberals. *Adelaide Walters Papers #4293, Southern Historical Collection, Wilson Library, University of North Carolina at Chapel Hill.*

In April 1961, Adelaide announced her reelection campaign. Remarking that Chapel Hill had recently "graduated from the status of a village to that of a city," she added, "The past four years on the board have provided an opportunity for me to become thoroughly acquainted with our local problems. My decision to run again for public office is based upon a desire to continue serving our expanding community." It wasn't a catchy campaign slogan, but it was sincere.

This go-round, she won more votes than any other single candidate. Paul Wager and Hubert Robinson were also reelected, and merchant Joe Page was elected to a two-year term. A new mayor was also chosen, Roland "Sandy" McClamroch.

At their next meeting, the aldermen elected Adelaide mayor pro tem for the ensuing two years. "If anyone had told me I was going to be a politician," she said with a laugh, "I would have been horrified!"

Her job was a balancing act. "We would like to keep approaches to Chapel Hill beautiful without interfering with business or real estate interests," she told the *Weekly*. "You can't legislate good taste. I sometimes wish you could."

Adelaide's educational background and leadership savvy came to the attention of Democratic governor Terry Sanford. He appointed her a member of the Commission to Study the Impact of State Sovereignty upon Financing of Local Governmental Services and Functions. She joked that it was "the longest title any committee ever had." Eventually, the committee submitted a report to the governor recommending ways that local governments, including the Town of Chapel Hill, could get tax relief on state-owned property like universities.

Adelaide also served on Governor Sanford's Commission on the Status of Women. It considered a broad range of issues affecting women, including state employment practices and policies; state labor laws; legal and property rights; and health, education and welfare programs. In the pages of the *Weekly*, Adelaide noted that modern technology gave women more free time and that "we would like to channel it in a constructive way." The governor valued female leadership. He believed that women "bring to state government an idealism of approach that we men sometimes overlook."

Managing to carve out some time at home with her husband and dog, Tar Baby, Adelaide enjoyed watching birds at her feeders. The hobby inspired more charity work. As a member of the Chapel Hill Bird Club, she helped keep track of local species. In December 1958, the group planned its annual "Christmas bird count" at University Lake. It was a cold and rainy day. Gathering beforehand at the Walters home for breakfast, many of the men looked for an excuse to back out. Adelaide—dressed in boots, trousers and a sweater—laughed at being afraid of a little rain. Her husband quipped, "Well, there *is* such a thing as reason." The group ended up going but took shelter on the porch of the custodian's building. Through a thirty-power glass, they spotted ducks, grebes, mergansers, herons and kingfishers.

ADELAIDE TREASURED FRANKLIN STREET's legendary Black "flower ladies." In 1962, while they faced opposition from a few merchants, the town manager reminded the aldermen of a 1930 ordinance prohibiting sales of garden products on the street. Adelaide defended the custom. "Even San Francisco allows it," she pointed out, adding that she enjoyed living in a community where people still appreciated flowers enough to buy them. Although she hoped to amend the ordinance, she couldn't do it alone. In the end, the Board of Aldermen gave the flower ladies an extended reprieve.

In 1963, Adelaide and six other local churchwomen founded the Inter-Church Council for Social Service (later the Inter-faith Council for Social Service). It addressed significant gaps in the community's social safety net. With no paid staff or office space, the council began providing crisis intervention assistance for those in dire need. One of its first efforts was helping a family whose home had been destroyed by fire. While insurance afforded a shell of a home, the council rounded up a stove, a refrigerator, a heater and other necessary furnishings.

IN THE SPRING OF 1963, Chapel Hill's desegregation battle resurfaced. Activists held demonstrations to raise awareness for a proposed ordinance banning segregation in restaurants, bars and motels. Although Adelaide wasn't keen on demonstrations, she did support the ordinance. In turn, white supremacists issued sharp rebukes. "If you should help vote enactment of the ordinance prohibiting segregation in Chapel Hill's public businesses, then Chapel Hill will have the dubious distinction of being the first town in North Carolina to do away with private rights," a constituent wrote to her in the summer of 1963 in a letter now archived at UNC's Wilson Library. "We are further along on the road to destruction of our democracy than is suspected."

On June 25, 1963, the Board of Aldermen gathered for a vote on this "public accommodations ordinance." Adelaide implored the others to muster the courage to support it. Most took the easy way out. Questioning the legal authority to pass such a law, they voted four to two to postpone action indefinitely. Adelaide and Alderman Robinson had been foiled.

At the next board meeting two weeks later, the police chief reported that the civil rights protests were stretching his officers to the breaking point. Alderman Giduz suggested beefing up the force's ranks. Adelaide quipped, "It might be cheaper to pass a public accommodations law."

A SECOND VOTE ON the ordinance was expected to take place on January 13, 1964. To rally support, a "Walk for Freedom" from Durham to Chapel Hill was held the previous day through sleet and freezing rain. Adelaide threw on her raincoat and joined in.

The following evening, the Board of Aldermen met at Town Hall for the big vote. With about one hundred citizens in attendance, the board began debate. Alderman Giduz expected that a public accommodations ordinance would be challenged in the Supreme Court of North Carolina. It was anyone's guess how the court would rule, he said, because there was no legal precedent. Then, Adelaide read from a prepared statement:

> *The underlying idea of a Public Accommodations Law is so simple that it was expressed in one sentence by the President of the United States, Lyndon Johnson, in his State of the Union message on January 9* [1964]: *"all members of the public should be given equal access to facilities open to the public." This statement seems reasonable to most people in Chapel Hill, since this is a university town where freedom flavors the spirit of a great university.*
>
> *It is likewise not surprising that Chapel Hillians are concerned that our Negro citizens often suffer personal embarrassment and shame from treatment in some public places here.*

We are aware that some 90 percent of our merchants subscribe to the principle of public accommodation. Indeed, the Merchants Association itself has gone on record in favor of open business for all citizens.

Why, then, is a Public Accommodations Law necessary? Why was the commandment "Thou shall not kill" ever put into law? It seems regrettable that we need legislation to enforce a plain truth. But because the bigotry of a few is poisoning the peace and harmony of community relationships, we are impelled to take action.

The Human Relations Committee set up by the Board of Aldermen and appointed by the Mayor, the Ministerial Association, as well as many individuals, have urged us to pass a Public Accommodations ordinance.

Some say that such an ordinance is an invasion of private property rights. Others point out that such rights have always been subject to the laws of the land—laws of ownership, sale, inheritance, zoning, sanitation, eminent domain.

For these reasons and many more, it is my hope that the Board of Aldermen will pass a Public Accommodations ordinance and thus in part restore the damaged public image of what I believe is an enlightened community.

Without missing a beat, Adelaide introduced an ordinance based on one enacted in Rockville, Maryland. She moved that the town attorney draft an ordinance along those lines, and Alderman Robinson seconded the motion. But then, things went off the rails. Alderman Giduz made a substitute motion that the mayor organize a mediation committee to "resolve racial differences that currently beset this town and to which complaints of racial discrimination could be brought." Adelaide insisted that such a committee would be "weak and ineffective without the ordinance to back it up." Regardless, after a vote, Giduz's substitute motion passed, four to two. Adelaide and Alderman Robinson had been foiled again.

As Adelaide predicted, the mayor's new committee got nowhere. So, in April 1964, she, her husband and two other concerned Chapel Hillians traveled to Washington, D.C. Citing Chapel Hill's racial situation, they lobbied Sam Ervin and other senators to pass the Civil Rights Act.

Three months later, on July 2, 1964, President Lyndon B. Johnson made history. He signed the Civil Rights Act into law, outlawing segregation in public places nationwide. We can only imagine the celebration at the Walters home that evening.

IN THE SPRING OF 1965, Adelaide ended her eight-year run as alderwoman. "With the Board itself, I've had a pleasant association," she remarked. "I have never felt that my being a woman makes a difference. Some, yes, but not a great deal."

Adelaide never turned her back on worthy causes. From 1964 to 1966, she was a member of the Advisory Commission on Intergovernmental Relations, created to "strengthen the American federal system and improve the ability of federal, state, and local governments to work together cooperatively, efficiently, and effectively."

About the time she hit sixty, her passion was providing affordable housing. In the late 1960s, shortly before her husband's death, she served on the mayor's Ad-Hoc Housing Committee. It researched possible sites for public housing. And from 1966 to 1973, she served as chairman of the Inter-faith Council for Social Services Housing Committee.

ON MAY 27, 1981, when Adelaide was seventy-four, her work was tragically cut short. On her way to the Raleigh-Durham airport, she was killed in a single-car crash into a tree. Also killed was Dame Eileen Younghusband, seventy-nine, a world-renowned pioneer of social work who was on a speaking tour of the United States. The driver of the car, retired child-relief worker Martha Branscombe, was seriously injured but survived.

After a year's recuperation, Martha partnered with the Inter-faith Council to complete one of Adelaide's pet projects.

Then, in April 1984, Martha proudly opened a twenty-four-unit affordable housing community for the elderly and people with disabilities on today's MLK Boulevard. She named it the Adelaide Walters Apartments. To selfless public servants like Adelaide, the gesture would have been more rewarding than a bronze statue.

5

THE WATER FLUORIDATION CONTROVERSY, 1951–64

The fluoridation of communal water supplies now is recognized
as a significant dental preventive measure.
—Dean John C. Brauer, UNC School of Dentistry

[Fluoridation is] *one of the greatest hoaxes in the history of medicine.*
—John Sprunt Hill, capitalist

In 1950, the streets of Chapel Hill were graced with hundreds of beautiful new shade trees and 180 desperately needed street markers. The next year, the Jaycee who made it all happen took on his next cause: fluoridating the local water supply. He was joining a national movement.

If anyone could get the ball rolling, it was handsome thirty-two-year-old Kenneth Putnam. Devoted to improving Chapel Hill, he had recently been crowned the village's "Young Man of the Year" and district vice-president of the Jaycees. He was also on the town's Board of Aldermen and was chairman of its Health Committee.

Putnam made his case to the board on November 26, 1951. He was well armed. With him was Dean John C. Brauer from UNC's new School of Dentistry and two public health officials, and Putnam had letters of endorsement from two area dental societies. Speaking on behalf of the dental school faculty, Dr. Brauer urged water fluoridation, declaring it safe and effective in reducing tooth decay in children. By meeting's end, the aldermen unanimously supported the measure.

In most North Carolina cities and towns, that would have sealed the deal. But in Chapel Hill, the university owned and operated the municipal water supply. For anything to happen on the fluoridation front, the university would have to approve it and pay for it. Instead, the university sat on it.

Dean Brauer waged his own public education campaign. On April 25, 1952, he published a long article in the *Chapel Hill Weekly*, beginning with this line: "The fluoridation of communal water supplies now is recognized as a significant dental preventive measure endorsed by the State, Nation, and World's outstanding dental, medical, and other scientific societies." He pointed to the growing list of North Carolina towns that had either approved or installed fluoridation equipment: Charlotte, Winston-Salem, Rocky Mount, Greensboro, Goldsboro, Concord, Dunn, Fayetteville, High Point, Lenoir, Reidsville, Roanoke Rapids, Rockingham, Salisbury, Southern Pines, Tarboro, Thomasville and Wilson.

The next year, Brauer shared the latest statistics: "The incidence of dental decay in children will be reduced at least 50% in those communities which have a water supply containing approximately one part per million of a fluoride."

By November 1953, a slew of local civic groups had unanimously adopted resolutions calling on the university to fluoridate. They included the Rotary Club, the Kiwanis Club, the Jaycees, the Community Council, the PTA and the local chapter of the American Association of University Women.

Regardless, as 1953 came to a close, there was radio silence from the university. Kenneth Putnam did the only thing he could. At the Board of Aldermen's meeting on February 22, 1954, he moved that it reaffirm its stand in favor of fluoridating the local water supply. The motion passed unanimously; again, the town manager forwarded a copy of the resolution to UNC's administration.

It wasn't until a year and a half later, on September 29, 1955, that the university finally broke its silence. Chancellor Robert B. House told the *Chapel Hill Weekly* that "the issue was closed for the present time and was not being submitted to the Board of Trustees for consideration." Period.

Declaring victory was conservative eighty-one-year-old capitalist John Sprunt Hill, a former UNC trustee. Like many Americans opposing fluoridation, he asserted that fluoride was a poison. University officials couldn't ignore his opinion, even if they wanted to. A capitalist with deep pockets, he gave UNC the Carolina Inn and contributed generously to the university library and other major projects. Claiming he personally beat back fluoridation the year before, he vowed to do so again if necessary.

"Why poison all the people in Chapel Hill for six or seven hundred children?" he asked. The *Chapel Hill Weekly* said some current UNC trustees had "thrown their influence against the process" as well.

The pro-fluoridation *Weekly* checked in with members of the local dental society. "I'm still as much in favor of it as the whole group has been," said Dr. William T. Burns. None of the dentists bought what Hill was selling.

In January 1956, as the university continued to dodge the issue, a revolutionary new toothpaste called Crest hit the market. The *Weekly* cited a ten-year study at Indiana University that proved Crest's "stannous fluoride" highly effective in preventing tooth decay. Chapel Hillians could run out and purchase a tube at the Village Pharmacy, the Carolina Pharmacy or Sutton's

Capitalist and conspiracy theorist John Sprunt Hill poured money into fighting fluoridation in Chapel Hill and Durham. *Courtesy of the State Archives of North Carolina.*

Drug Store. But there was a caveat, researchers warned: "The tooth-paste is no substitute for community water fluoridation."

In May 1957, after serving two terms as alderman, Kenneth Putnam lost his race for a third. Fluoridation had lost one of its strongest advocates.

The *Weekly* did what it could. In cooperation with the North Carolina Dental Society, the paper repeated the scientific view that "fluoridation is an effective and safe procedure for substantial reduction of dental decay." In solid agreement were the American Dental Association, the American Medical Association, the U.S. Public Health Service and the National Research Council. But Chapel Hill eccentric Manning Simons fretted about unknown health risks. He ran a large advertisement in an area newspaper that claimed, "Dentists as a group are not competent authorities concerning the effect of fluorides on any part of the body other than the teeth." Biochemists were the *real* experts, he said, listing some of them who opposed fluoridation.

As the 1950s ended—more than eight years after the Board of Aldermen and the dental school first recommended fluoridation— UNC's administration continued to hedge. Perhaps fluoridation was too controversial nationwide to touch. Some argued that fluoridation was unconstitutional, an infringement on individual rights or just plain too expensive. If the university supported the measure, would students leave en masse? Would UNC's support dissuade many students from applying for admission? And would UNC lose vital funding from the state legislature and private donors?

On April 11, 1960, the aldermen went through the motions once again. They unanimously endorsed fluoridation of the municipal water supply and urged the university to act. This time, the administration opened the door a crack. It agreed to survey 6,200 water customers on the issue.

John Sprunt Hill declared war. He wrote and financed a media blitz. One of his full-page ads in the *Weekly* featured the headline, "Fluoridation of Water—Conceived in Iniquity and Born in Sin." He asserted that fluoridated water was first used in Russian gulags to "dull the minds of prisoners and steadily weaken their bodies." He also contended that water fluoridation was a secret plot by aluminum manufacturers to sell their waste products. According to one report, Hill called fluoridation a "Russian move to wipe out the American people, perhaps sterilize them, or cause in them increased heart trouble." He wasn't the only American raising the specter of a Communist plot.

On May 31, 1960, the day after Hill ran his advertisement, the university's survey results were in. By a three-to-one margin, they favored fluoridation. The very next day, the university announced plans to fluoridate the town's water by October 1, 1960. The decision was backed by Chancellor William B. Aycock, Business Manager J. Arthur Branch and President Bill Friday. They ordered the fluoridation equipment. Finally, the town could put this fight in the rearview mirror.

Not so fast, thought Manning Simons. Known for supporting conservative causes, he announced plans in mid-June 1960 to seek a court injunction to halt fluoridation. Local newspaperman Roland Giduz later described Simons this way:

> He claimed to have been "an escaped lunatic" who came to Chapel Hill from a Richmond asylum in 1936. His personal trademarks were wearing earmuffs almost year-round, walking wherever he wanted to go—because he enjoyed walking, and asking questions, questions, questions constantly. He'd remember every syllable of your answers….Ask him a question and you'll most likely get a question in reply. And more than likely the question will be "Why do you ask that?"

If Simons was an oddball, he was no conspiracy theorist. On August 18, 1960, his lawyer, W. Harold Edwards, filed a complaint in the Orange

County Superior Court, asking for a mandatory injunction to stop the university from fluoridating the town's water supply. Simons argued that fluoridation was a "yet unproved experiment in mass medication" and that those opposed to it would be forced to drink that water. UNC canceled the order for fluoridation equipment.

By early fall 1960, the state attorney general had agreed to represent the university in the case. In October 1961, after more than a year of delays, a judge struck eighteen allegations from Simons's complaint and denied twenty-six others. That December, after further delays, word came that the case would finally be heard, in March 1962. But when March rolled around, Giduz—an alderman elected in 1957 and Chapel Hill's "Young Man of the Year" in 1960—discovered that the trial had not even been scheduled for the current session.

Manning Simons fought fluoridation in the courts, asserting that it constituted "mass medication." *Roland Giduz Photographic Collection #P0033, North Carolina Collection Photographic Archives, Louis Round Wilson Special Collections Library, University of North Carolina at Chapel Hill.*

When the Board of Aldermen met on the evening of March 27, 1962, this scholarly writer-editor was at no loss for words. Calling the dispute between Simons and the university a "farce," Giduz declared, "We have an obligation to practice what we preach, and we've been preaching fluoridation. The UNC dental faculty has advised fluoridation, but the university, which pays them, has not practiced what it preaches." He accused UNC of being "laggardly" in pushing the case, noting, "The plaintiff is winning the case by default." He urged his fellow aldermen to reiterate their support for fluoridation. Passing a resolution to that effect (for the fourth time), they instructed the town manager and town attorney to confer with UNC officials and urge fluoridation, once and for all.

The following month, the aldermen learned that the recent delay in bringing the case to trial was due to illness in the attorney general's office. It was overworked and undermanned. What else could go wrong?

Assistant Attorney General James Bullock got an idea. Hoping for the earliest possible disposition of the case, he requested that the Executive

Committee of UNC's Board of Trustees formally approve the fluoridation measure. They complied. Nevertheless, in August 1962, higher-ups at the university stated that they would wait until the Simons suit was settled before proceeding with fluoridation.

"Preposterous," huffed Giduz, alleging that university officials were "abdicating their authority." After all, the suit had not resulted in an injunction against the university. Giduz feared the suit would "be in court for years and years" and that fluoridation would be forgotten. Looking the other aldermen in the eye, he said, "I think the Town should try to make the University live up to its obligations."

A student of political science, Giduz took charge. On the evening of September 17, 1962, he called together thirty-five allies at Town Hall, including attorney Robert Cooper and about fifteen local dentists. They formed the Chapel Hill Citizens' Fluoridation Committee. Cooper explained the legal strategy: the committee would file amicus briefs to help the judge reach the desired decision in the Simons case. Giduz divvied up tasks. While Cooper researched legal precedents, the dentists—including Drs. Theodore Oldenburg, William T. Burns and Ray Burns—would gather scientific data on the benefits of fluoridated water. William Straughn, Floy Oldham and others would conduct fundraising for legal expenses. By evening's end, the men had shaken hands on the plan.

A few days later, committee secretary Dr. Ray Burns offered some comic relief. His two-year-old son, Mark, had eaten the notes from the meeting. But it was no major loss. Cooper kept plugging away at his brief for presentation in court.

In December 1962, Giduz made a desperate appeal for funds to defray legal expenses. "We need contributions in any amount," he stated, "and we need them now." The court was scheduled to hear the Manning Simons case in Hillsborough on January 21, 1963.

Unfortunately, Giduz's committee was in for another letdown. Simons's attorney asked for a delay until March for "personal reasons." It seemed Simons was simply running out the clock.

Meanwhile, Harvard nutrition expert Dr. Frederick J. Stare arrived in Chapel Hill to preach the gospel of fluoridation. Addressing UNC's School of Public Health, he stated, "Fluoride is recognized as an essential mineral nutrient—needed for the development of tough tooth enamel to fight decay." He asserted that enriching water with fluoride was an important nutritive process, just like enriching salt with iodine. "I am surprised to see that Chapel Hill is behind Bogota, Colombia," he quipped, explaining that fluoride was recently introduced into that third-world country's water supply.

On March 1, 1963, a decision was finally handed down in the Manning Simons case. Judge Hamilton Hobgood of the Orange County Superior Court threw the case out on a technicality. "This is the most significant step toward getting the water supply fluoridated in the thirty-months history of the case," Giduz remarked to the *Weekly*. "We certainly appreciate the attorney general taking action as he pledged he would, after such a long delay. I'm certainly very pleased and I know all the members of the committee are, too."

But it wasn't over yet. Manning Simons's attorney announced that he would appeal to the Supreme Court of North Carolina. They were granted three extensions to file the appeal but each time missed the deadline.

At long last, on September 3, 1963, Judge James Latham of the Chatham County Superior Court dismissed the case. It had been delayed far too long, he opined, adding, "With things at this stage of the game, it would be ten years before the case got to the jury."

Manning Simons simply refused to give up. His lawyer said he planned to "start over" with a new suit.

Enough is enough, thought Chancellor Aycock. He promptly ordered the fluoridation equipment at a cost of about $64,000. On September 10, 1963, he told the *Weekly*, "We're going to fluoridate unless we're stopped."

For Chapel Hillians on both sides of the issue, the final months of 1963 were nail-biters. While the equipment was expected to arrive in mid-December and take at least two weeks to get up and running, no one knew if Manning Simons had any more tricks up his sleeve.

Then, in February 1964, Chapel Hill became the forty-eighth city in North Carolina with fluoridated water flowing from its taps. While Giduz and the other pro-fluoridation forces declared sweet victory, they never lost sight of the real winners: the children.

THE DESEGREGATION BATTLE ON THE HILL

It's called a liberal place, but that's a mirage, man.
When you go to get water, you just get a mouthful of sand.
—Harold Foster, Black student activist

In the early 1960s, Chapel Hill's reputation as the "Southern fortress of liberality" was shattered. Civil rights activists were kicked, poked with cattle prods and doused with bleach and ammonia. Police arrested hundreds of peaceful protesters. Merchants with "Whites Only" signs doubled down. When the Board of Aldermen rejected a nondiscrimination ordinance, activists staged an eight-day fast in front of the post office. The Ku Klux Klan condemned the fasters at a rally and cross-burning on the outskirts of town. Where would it all end?

FIRST, LET'S SEE HOW it all began. In Greensboro on February 1, 1960, four Black male students from North Carolina A&T University walked into a Woolworths, sat down at the lunch counter and politely asked for service. They were refused. Although a billy club–toting policeman told them to leave, they sat peacefully until closing time. Due to the publicity surrounding the event, these courageous men went down in history as the "Greensboro Four."

Students at Chapel Hill's all-Black Lincoln High School were electrified by the news. They had lived their entire lives under the dehumanizing yoke of racism and Jim Crow segregation. Now, a youth-led sit-in movement was blazing across the South. Finally, there was hope.

A reporter from the *Chapel Hill Weekly* interviewed students in the Lincoln High cafeteria. Segregation simply must end, they said. Harold Foster, senior class vice-president, three-letter athlete and editor of the school newspaper, believed in the promise of freedom. "There should be integration," he said, "if we are to live according to the law of the land and to substantiate what President Lincoln said in the Gettysburg Address." Cryptically, he added, "We have a 'rebuttal' planned to take place before the next paper comes out. You may have front page news for Monday."

ON THE EVENING OF Sunday, February 28, 1960, Harold and eight other students were ready to make their move. They entered the Colonial Drug

Store, which they often patronized at 450 West Franklin Street. After making purchases at the counter, they sat down in a whites-only booth. Owner "Big John" Carswell swooped in, insisting the boys leave. They refused. Police escorted them out of the store, and they were later convicted of trespassing. History would remember them as the "Chapel Hill Nine."

Harold Foster was just getting started. That night, he and several fellow students made protest signs for the following day.

According to plan, Harold led seventy-five to one hundred Lincoln High School students in a double-file picket line at Colonial Drug. They demanded "equal service," he told a *Daily Tar Heel* reporter, adding that they would continue "indefinitely…until we get what we are after." Chapel Hill was stunned.

Harold Foster was likened to a "hot spark plug" for the local freedom movement. *Jim Wallace Photographic Collection, University Libraries, University of North Carolina at Chapel Hill.*

BORN IN 1942, HAROLD Foster grew up poor in the town's Pottersfield section, the heart of the Black community. He was shaped by a painful childhood memory. Once, his mother severely punished him for something he didn't do. The episode branded him a rebel, he explained, challenging "whatever was said, and whatever was put down as edict." Combined with his broad base of support and knack for organization, he had all the right stuff to fight segregation head-on.

On March 1, 1960, a mass meeting was held at the "Negro Community Center" (today's Hargraves Center). The crowd formed a local protest organization called the Chapel Hill–Carrboro Committee for Racial Equality. Seen as a rising star in the local freedom movement, Harold Foster was elected chairman. He was also appointed to an executive committee along with Charlie Jones, the white minister of the liberal Community Church. "What you are trying to do is right," Charlie told the students. "It will take level-headed thinking, calm action, and cannot be done by explosion. But it's right." By meeting's end, the youths had a path forward. With support and guidance from white and Black adults, they would employ orderly action and negotiations in the Black business district. Nonviolence was their byword.

Chapel Hill got eight inches of snow the next day, so Harold postponed the picketing. He feared it would be too easy for his opponents to bombard the students with snowballs—and maybe too easy to justify fighting back.

The picketers were back on March 7, pacing silently in front of the Dairy Bar and Colonial Drug. One of the picket signs read, "We are united for dignity and equality." Another one read, "All we ask for is justice." Police Chief William Blake feared racial violence, but it didn't materialize.

The picketers followed strict guidelines. They had to attend two hours of "picket school" and take a vow of nonviolence. They also had to dress neatly, avoid blocking entrance doors and limit themselves to fifteen to twenty at a time. To further guard against violence, Harold notified the police of protests in advance and planned to wrap things up before dark. But that didn't keep the students from being labeled "troublemakers."

Despite the almost daily picketing at Colonial Drug, proprietor John Carswell was defiant. He insisted that he would follow "local custom" and refused to negotiate. The battle lines were drawn.

Another freak snowstorm hit Chapel Hill on March 9, so Harold and his team halted the picketing again. As soon as the snow melted, they were back at it.

Late that month, the picketers called off action at the Dairy Bar. Management had removed the booths and stools, reported the *Weekly*, offering equal stand-up service for all. The Village Pharmacy followed suit at its lunch counter. The picketers refocused their ire on Colonial Drug. Perhaps Carswell would surrender for fear of losing his large Black customer base.

Black students picket at the Dairy Bar on West Franklin Street, early March 1960. *Roland Giduz Photographic Collection #P0033, North Carolina Collection Photographic Archives, Louis Round Wilson Special Collections Library, University of North Carolina at Chapel Hill.*

A month later, however, he was as stubborn as ever. Harold tried another strategy. He posted two activists outside Colonial Drug, urging customers to boycott the store. The leaflets noted that "Negroes are invited into Colonial Drug Store for drugs and are treated fairly, but when Negroes buy food they must stand while others sit"—a practice that was "unfair, undemocratic, and unChristian." Reportedly, half of Carswell's Black customers took their business elsewhere.

During this period, the mayor's Human Relations Committee negotiated with segregated restaurants in the *white* business district. Although a few of them agreed to serve UNC's handful of Black students, most remained completely segregated.

On May 8, 1960, Martin Luther King Jr. encouraged Chapel Hill's student activists to keep up the pressure. *From right to left*: Lonita Terrell Whitted, Reverend Charlie Jones, Martin Luther King Jr., Harold Foster and Hilliard Caldwell. Presumably, the man at far left is Joe Straley. *John Kenyon Chapman Papers #5441, Southern Historical Collection, Wilson Library, University of North Carolina at Chapel Hill.*

Some whites mobilized to maintain the status quo. Picketer David Dansby Jr., soon to become the first Black undergraduate to earn a degree from UNC, received threatening phone calls and had cherry bombs placed at his door. Some protesters were intimidated by their white employers. There are even stories of white-robed Klansmen terrorizing the Black youngsters as they walked home at night.

By mid- to late April 1960, the Committee for Racial Equality was getting pressure from all sides—even from its liberal white advisors—to abandon picketing in favor of peaceful negotiations. The Executive Committee voted to halt the picketing. They began using leaflets to seek support for desegregation.

On May 8, Martin Luther King Jr. arrived in Chapel Hill to deliver four speeches over two days. His first appearance was later that day at the Negro Community Center. A crowd of about four hundred showed up, including many Lincoln High School students. First, Harold announced another leaflet in production. It called for boycotts of establishments that refused equal service to all. Then, after introductions, Dr. King stepped up to the microphone. In part, he said:

You are demonstrating a magnificent act, a magnificent act of non-cooperation with the forces of evil. You are not seeking to put stores that practice discrimination out of business. You are seeking to put justice in business. Tell the businessman, "You respect our dollars, now respect our persons." Continue to struggle until we can really obtain democracy in all its dimensions and everybody in the community will be able to live together as brothers.

Dr. King's visit to town culminated at Hill Hall on May 9, 1960. Addressing an overflow crowd, he reminded followers of his central message: "There must be no violence in the struggle for racial equality." That struggle—in Chapel Hill and around the country—quieted down for a time. Harold Foster was left to fight another day.

IN EARLY JANUARY 1961, a hit musical with an all-Black cast came to the all-white Carolina Theatre on Franklin Street. It was *Porgy and Bess*, starring Sidney Poitier, Dorothy Dandridge and Pearl Bailey. A teacher at the Black high school wanted to take her class to see the film. She asked the Chapel Hill Ministerial Association to negotiate with theater manager Carrington Smith for an integrated showing. Smith refused, explaining that white patrons would object. Local dramatist Paul Green also appealed to Smith but got nowhere. As a compromise, Smith offered to reserve the last Saturday night showing of the film for "Negroes only." The association declined the offer, and eleven members announced that they would boycott the theater. Picketing began on January 6 by a group soon calling itself the Citizens Committee for Open Movies.

Reverend Charlie Jones served as picketing organizer. Before long, his roster of about two hundred volunteers included UNC professors Wayne Bowers, Daniel Pollitt and Joe Straley; a virtual army of university and high school students; and Harold Foster, now a freshman English major commuting to North Carolina College in Durham (North Carolina Central University).

Concerned about the potential for violence, the police chief posted an extra officer in sight of the Carolina Theatre and the Varsity Theater across the street. On January 10, two white UNC students heckled the picketers.

The Citizens Committee for Open Movies did more than picket. It assembled a biracial team, including Reverend Charlie Jones, to negotiate with theater managers. In mid-January 1961, the Carolina's manager stated

The biracial Citizens Committee for Open Movies pickets the Carolina Theatre in January 1961. On the site today is Top of the Hill Restaurant. *Roland Giduz Photographic Collection #P0033, North Carolina Collection Photographic Archives, Louis Round Wilson Special Collections Library, University of North Carolina at Chapel Hill.*

that he would remain segregated in "the best interest of the community." The Varsity's manager had the same bottom line, saying that he "decided not to depart from our long-standing policy on admissions." Picketing began there on February 6.

Local NAACP worker Hilliard Caldwell helped organize a show of support for the theater campaign. With a police escort, he led about sixty Blacks on a march down Franklin Street, singing hymns. They stopped in front of Town Hall on Rosemary Street, praying for an end to racial discrimination in all public places.

It seemed like a major breakthrough when the Varsity agreed to integrate if the Carolina did first. But the Carolina's manager was unmoved. Theaters are in business to make money, he said, and picketing didn't hurt his box office sales one bit. Integration, on the other hand, was risky. Whites could commit violence at the theater or withdraw their patronage altogether.

Violence soon erupted outside the Varsity. A white UNC graduate student was "knocked down and beaten by two white youths," though not seriously. A few days later, another graduate student was attacked after leaving his picketing shift.

Meanwhile, the Citizens Committee scheduled a meeting with William Enloe, the district manager of the Carolina Theatre's parent company. The committee was ready to prove majority support for integrating the theaters. On the morning of March 27, 1961, the *Chapel Hill Weekly* reported:

> *The citizens committee plans to present the movie chain representative a letter signed by eleven ministers supporting integration, a newspaper advertisement signed by 350 University professors, a petition signed by high school students, a newspaper advertisement signed by graduate students in the UNC Political Science Department, the results of a survey of 1,800 UNC students showing 87 per cent willing to accept theater integration and 70 per cent requesting a change in admissions policy, letters from church groups, a copy of a resolution passed by the UNC Student Legislature urging "equality of service," along with a report on integration in restaurants, the public library at UNC and in the public schools, in churches, and in various other activities.*

The Enloe meeting had mixed results. He vowed to integrate eventually, adding, "But I don't know if it will be 1961 or even 1981." His one condition was that he not be threatened. The Citizens Committee halted picketing at the Carolina.

During the university's summer break, Chapel Hill seemed like a ghost town. The theater integration campaign was on hold.

As soon as classes resumed that fall, the Carolina Theatre conducted an experiment. It quietly began admitting Black UNC students with a valid student ID. Since only about a dozen Blacks were enrolled at the time, Black townspeople condemned the policy. Nevertheless, on August 17, 1961, Black students Ann Douglas and Edith Mayfield attended a screening of *The Dark at the Top of the Stairs*. The theater manager proclaimed it the first time a "picture theater" in North Carolina admitted Blacks.

THAT OCTOBER, THE CITIZENS Committee huddled for a strategy session. A member reported on a recent meeting with William Enloe. "My impression," he said, "was that Mr. Enloe wants to take this very, very gradually." One suggestion was to phase in integration by issuing fifty ID cards to local Blacks in November, one hundred cards in December and hopefully start full integration right after the holidays. Someone else piped up, calling the card proposal "another way of gradualism, and gradualism stinks." The room erupted with applause. To round out the evening, a new, sixteen-member Executive Committee was elected, to include Harold Foster. He was officially back in the game.

A few days later, the Citizens Committee sent a letter to the Varsity's manager, Andy Gutierrez. Requesting a meeting on November 7, the letter said, in part:

> *Nine months have passed since we made our first request that you open your theater to all the citizens of Chapel Hill without discrimination. Since that time, the election of members in the Board of Education with a mandate to desegregate the public schools has resulted in desegregation of every public school in Chapel Hill.*

The Gutierrez meeting took place as planned. This time, he said he had to consult the stockholders of the theater's parent company. It seemed like just one more delaying tactic. The committee accused him of "repeatedly blocking every attempt to integrate" and refusing to cooperate in any way. When the meeting was over, a negotiator took him aside, saying, "You know, of course, what this means."

"I guess it means picketing," Gutierrez sheepishly replied. Indeed, picketing was resumed there on a nightly basis.

The Varsity's stockholders agreed to the same limited desegregation policy as the Carolina. Picketing at the Varsity was halted. Then, in December, the Varsity desegregated completely.

The Carolina took another baby step. It allowed Black students to bring members of their families or nonstudent dates and allowed white patrons to bring a Black guest. Then, in March 1962, the Carolina went all the way, too.

It had taken about a year to change the hearts and minds of Chapel Hill's theater managers. Other business owners, however, would prove much tougher to crack.

AS THE SUN BROKE the horizon on April 5, 1963, two white UNC students began picketing the College Café across Franklin Street from the Carolina

Coffee Shop. They were Pat Cusick and John Dunne with the Student Peace Union. Pat's sign read, "Land of the Free—For Whom?" John's read, "1863–1963: How Long Must Americans Wait for a Cup of Coffee?" These young men were sparking a new era of protest in Chapel Hill.

A policeman walked toward them. "You boys planning to picket long?"

"Only until he integrates," Pat quipped.

Surprisingly, the College Café protest backfired. Customers came in droves, as fraternities dared their pledges to break the picket line. The place actually ran out of food. One of the owners wryly thanked the picketers for padding his pockets and invited them to come back the next day.

John Dunne, civil rights activist and Morehead scholar, circa 1964. *John Ehle Papers #4555, Southern Historical Collection, Wilson Library, University of North Carolina at Chapel Hill.*

Just days later, massive civil rights demonstrations erupted in Birmingham, Alabama, where police were locking up hundreds of Black protesters. John Dunne put down his picket sign, hopped in a Volkswagen van with a student journalist and sped south.

Born in Boston, John spent his early years in Ohio. He graduated from the Choate School in Connecticut with high honors, including the School Seal Prize in recognition of his leadership, scholarship and character. Voted "the straightest arrow" by his senior class, he played fullback on the football team and was first violinist in the orchestra. Both Harvard and UNC offered him scholarships. He chose UNC. He wanted to learn all about the South and its challenges.

As that Volkswagen van rolled into Birmingham, armed whites stood together in groups. John learned that Blacks were attending daily mass meetings at the churches. Before he knew it, he was listening to Black preachers like Martin Luther King Jr., Ralph Abernathy and James Bevel. They endorsed Gandhi's philosophy of nonviolence as if it was a religion.

During John's mission in the city, he overheard a crime in progress, one of unspeakable racial hatred and violence. A "little Negro girl," he began,

had her head beaten in with a brick behind the Motel while her crippled older sister on crutches stood by helpless and watched the child thrown into a car and carried away to be dumped somewhere along a lonely Alabama road—

this was never reported, no one but the girl, the killer, myself and five or six others at the Motel and several neighbors who heard the screaming and the car, plus the two policemen who were dispatched to "investigate," and left without even asking questions of those of us involved. But I will never forget the face of the girl, hysterical, sobbing uncontrollably, "They've killed my sister."

One afternoon, John walked down to the jail, where countless Black schoolchildren were being held. Hundreds of parents were holding a twenty-four-hour vigil on the square. He explained:

They had heard the rumors that kids were being killed inside, so they were worried sick. I tried to raise their spirits. At that time prisoners were being bonded out at the rate of about sixteen an hour, and I tried to help them find their parents and get a bus back to town. Several jail wardens saw me and got very irritated. I guess I wasn't hard to see, for I was the only white person there.

On trumped-up charges of loitering and resisting arrest, John was thrown in jail. One of his cellmates was a Klansman who'd been out "shooting at Negroes."

John made bail, and the charges were later dropped. Boarding a plane back to Chapel Hill, he realized that Birmingham had changed him forever. Segregation and its attendant sins simply couldn't stand.

PAT CUSICK WAS REELING from the College Café fiasco. To him, racial discrimination in Chapel Hill was "an intolerable insult to the spirit of a free university and to the fundamental precepts of freedom and human dignity." Thirty-two years old with a stocky build, Pat was "deep, deep, deep in the closet." He was born and raised in Alabama, where his great-grandfather had been a slaveholder and founded a local unit of the KKK. Pat first realized segregation was "screwed up" while attending a Benedictine high school, where priests argued that it was morally wrong. He was further enlightened in the U.S. Air Force, he said, since his Black supervisor was "brighter than I was." After attending Belmont Abbey College near Charlotte, he transferred to UNC in 1961. In December 1962, he and John Dunne organized the campus chapter of the Student Peace Union. It quickly focused on desegregating Chapel Hill.

By this point, Pat had considered assembling a broader organization. "Man, this town is hard to crack," warned Harold Foster. "It's called a liberal place, but that's a mirage, man. When you go to get water, you just get a mouthful of sand." Regardless, he and Pat reached out to their respective communities, and on May 3, 1963, about sixty people met at St. Joseph's "Colored" Methodist Episcopal Church to organize the Committee for Open Business (COB). Harold's admirers urged him to take the lead. Stepping before the crowd, he announced: "We are here tonight to find out what happened to the integration spirit of 1960. The Negro community must let the people of Chapel Hill know they are ready for equality and want a community with equality—in toto." Taking his turn at the podium, Pat imagined "a community in which a person may be served in any establishment without regard to the color of his skin."

No one knew how many segregated establishments the town actually had. A classic example, however, was the Oh Boy! Drive-In restaurant at Church and Rosemary Streets. With "colored" carhops or "curb boys," the burger joint was a popular hangout for white high school students. On the other side of town was a family restaurant called Brady's and its soft-serve stand, Frozen Kustard.

SHORTLY AFTER THE COB organized, a twelve-member steering committee was appointed, to include Harold Foster and Pat Cusick. Harold was made co-chairman. Enlisting a negotiation team and a slew of picketers, the group unleashed an all-out assault on the College Café. This time, the eatery's patronage quickly dropped off.

Meanwhile, horrific images from Birmingham were indelibly etched into the nation's consciousness. Under the rein of police commissioner and white supremacist Bull Connor, officers besieged Black demonstrators with vicious guard dogs and high-velocity fire hoses. Some Chapel Hillians feared that their own town verged on mass violence. On May 19, 1963, twenty local ministers asked Mayor McClamroch to appoint a committee to work toward integrating the town's restaurants, bars and motels through peaceful negotiation. Their letter said, in part:

> *Recent non-violent mass protests in Birmingham, Alabama, Nashville, Tennessee, Raleigh and Greensboro, North Carolina, underscore the deep frustration and feeling of hopelessness among Negroes in the South over the denial to them of full rights and privileges enjoyed by white citizens.*
>
> *Despite progress in Chapel Hill…we believe that the same frustration and hopelessness exists in both Negro and white citizens of Chapel Hill who feel*

the hurt of segregation. We would regret if such persons would feel it was necessary to engage in mass protests to make further progress in Chapel Hill.

We believe these rights and privileges ought to be freely granted not because they are forced from us, but because they are just. We, therefore, request that you form a committee…charged with the responsibility of without further delay removing all policies in both government and business which deny rights and services because of race.

Soon, Mayor McClamroch appointed citizens to his Integration Committee. To Harold and Pat, things were looking up.

THE BLACK STUDENTS WERE itching to stage a march. At the COB's meeting on May 22, 1963, a march was scheduled for the following Saturday at two o'clock. They rehearsed freedom songs like "We Shall Overcome" and "Give Me That Old Freedom Spirit."

The next evening, it seemed there might be a legislative solution to the whole thing. UNC sociology professor Don Irish suggested that the Board of Aldermen pass a "public accommodations ordinance." It would assure reasonable service to *all* citizens in public places—now. The community began debating the idea.

Meanwhile, owners of a few segregated businesses considered integrating. The proprietor of a bowling alley and snack bar, All-Star Lanes, heard that the march would be going all the way out to his establishment at Eastgate Shopping Center. "You needn't do that," he told the COB's negotiation committee. "We plan to integrate in the fall."

"That's fine," they replied, "we won't need to march out there *in the fall*."

The day before the march, the manager of the bowling alley called back. He said the marchers really shouldn't bother coming out to his place, because he planned to integrate in about a month. The response on the line was, "Fine, we won't march out to your place *in about a month*."

ON SATURDAY, MAY 25, 1963, about 350 protesters gathered at St. Joseph's Church and marched east down Franklin Street. Among them were Black high school and college students, white UNC students and clergy of both races. Their banner featured Martin Luther King Jr.'s slogan, "Freedom Now." It was Harold Foster's finest hour. John Dunne walked alongside the column, leading it in song:

We shall overcome.
We shall overcome.
We shall overcome someday.
Deep in my heart,
I do believe,
We shall overcome someday.

The marchers paused along the route, pointing out segregated businesses: Leo's Restaurant, Colonial Drug, West Franklin Street Luncheonette and College Café. The column turned north on Henderson Street, then west on Rosemary. On reaching Town Hall at Columbia Street, it slowed to a halt. Charlie Jones climbed the steps and faced the crowd. "Do you want your freedom?" he shouted.

The Committee for Open Business held its first march on May 25, 1963. Harold Foster is at far right. *Roland Giduz Photographic Collection #P0033, North Carolina Collection Photographic Archives, Louis Round Wilson Special Collections Library, University of North Carolina at Chapel Hill.*

"Yes!" the crowd shouted back.

Jones condemned the snail's pace of integration since the 1954 *Brown v. Board of Education* decision. "The reason we must protest is because there is no movement," he added. "We must protest for two words, two words that are now ringing across the South. They are 'now' and 'all.'" He said the Board of Aldermen could immediately enact desegregation by refusing business licenses to segregated establishments. "There is only one other way for us…to keep saying we want our freedom, nonviolently and constantly," he said. "Will you do it?"

"Yes!" the crowd roared. Marching onward in song, the protesters coursed their way back to St. Joseph's Church. On their arrival, Harold Foster had exciting news. Earlier that day, two local businesses capitulated: All-Star Lanes and the Oh Boy! Drive-In restaurant. More cheers rang out from the crowd. Their pressure campaign was beginning to pay off.

THE LOCAL FREEDOM MOVEMENT got another boost when John and Pat crossed paths with a well-trained, well-connected civil rights activist. At a mass meeting in Durham, they met twenty-year-old Quinton Baker, the Black, gay head of the NAACP chapter at North Carolina College (North Carolina Central University). Just days earlier, he had led a sit-in outside a Howard Johnson's between Durham and Chapel Hill with over seven hundred students and organized a one-thousand-people-strong march through the

Quinton Baker leads a practice protest march in the summer of 1963. Harold Foster follows directly behind. *Jim Wallace Photographic Collection, University Libraries, University of North Carolina at Chapel Hill.*

110

streets of Durham. John knew an opportunity when he saw one. He lured Quinton to Chapel Hill and into the COB to help train new members. The two men began an intimate relationship. As it matured, Quinton became a key tactician in the town's desegregation effort.

Bright and articulate, Quinton grew up in Greenville, North Carolina, where he worked as a shoeshine boy. He first discovered the pain of segregation as a teenager when he was denied tickets to a concert. By high school, his leadership abilities were undeniable. During his senior year, he was elected to six official positions, including student body president. He graduated with honors. On entering college, he poured his heart and soul into the student-led freedom movement.

Unfortunately, the mayor's Integration Committee failed in its negotiations with segregated businesses. Its members concluded that a public accommodations ordinance was the only way to achieve an "open city." But the Merchants Association vehemently opposed the ordinance. It issued this statement: "Businessmen should not be picketed, coerced or threatened by any means."

Harold Foster and other COB members didn't let that stop them from picketing Colonial Drug. They were out to make an example of John Carswell. He was a formidable foe. He ran a full-page ad in the *Weekly*, insisting he'd never surrender to intimidation or coercion. He threatened the picketers, muttering, "I'm going to get you." They didn't take him lightly. Whenever they showed up outside his store, he placed a pistol on his countertop for "cleaning." One day, according to the *Weekly*, he "sat in his store entranceway with a loaded pistol in his hand, threatening to shoot any nigger who came too close."

During this period, the COB occasionally picketed Leo's Restaurant on West Franklin Street and Brady's Restaurant on East Franklin. They refused to desegregate, claiming they would lose too much business.

On May 31, 1963, just six days after the COB's first march, the College Café announced "the lowering of racial bars." But that didn't mean the movement was turning the corner. Signs of racial unrest were on the rise across the South.

On June 18, 1963, North Carolinians tuned their black-and-white television sets to an official statement by Governor Terry Sanford. Worried about the potential for racial violence, he insisted that all demonstrations cease throughout the state. Segregationists must consent to negotiations.

John Carswell flatly refused. Picketing only made him *more* determined. "I'm not going to change," he told a *Weekly* reporter. "They can walk out there until doomsday." With intransigence on all sides, the activists pinned their hopes on the public accommodations ordinance.

Then, on the evening of June 25, 1963, anxious Chapel Hillians on both sides of the issue crowded into Town Hall for the Board of Aldermen's vote on the proposal. If passed, it would end all segregation in area restaurants, bars and motels—the first of its kind in the state. Harold Foster fidgeted in his seat. Would the aldermen assuage his race's pain and humiliation? Or was freedom an impossible dream?

Joe Augustine with the Merchants Association rose from his chair. While condemning "discriminatory policies," he complained that the ordinance wouldn't give a person a choice. An insurance man said, "I believe a man has a constitutional right to discriminate." Impassioned pleas lasted for nearly two hours. "Negroes want dignity just like anybody else," one man said politely. "Please consider that when it comes time to vote." Harold couldn't have said it better himself.

During a mass demonstration on July 4, 1963, protesters including Harold Foster (*foreground, center*) point out the segregated College Café. *Jim Wallace Photographic Collection, University Libraries, University of North Carolina at Chapel Hill.*

When the issue finally went to the board, Alderman Paul Wager moved that it be postponed indefinitely. The majority concurred in a four-to-two vote. Favoring the original proposal were Hubert Robinson Sr., Chapel Hill's first Black alderman; and Adelaide Walters, its first female alderman. They were outvoted by Roland Giduz, Joe Page, Gene Strowd and Paul Wager, who carefully sidestepped the issue.

As disappointed as Harold was, he didn't let up for a second. "If lawmakers can't pass laws to protect Negro citizens," he told the *Weekly*, "then the Negro has to seek other alternatives to gain his freedom and to destroy this system which crushes him."

Indeed, the COB took its fight to the next level. A higher law required it, members said. Pat Cusick began leading workshops in mass nonviolent civil disobedience. In case demonstrators ever faced arrest, they were taught to go limp, so as to neither help nor hinder the police.

On July 4, 1963, the COB held a march with about five hundred people joining in. It was touted as Chapel Hill's largest march to date. But the community's patience for demonstrations was wearing thin. Although the *Weekly*'s editor claimed to be "in complete sympathy with the Negro's struggle for full equality," he denounced the COB for making the town "another center of racial strife and turmoil." COB members knew pressure campaigns didn't guarantee victories, but they were convinced that victories were impossible without them.

HAROLD FOSTER AND HIS Executive Committee picked their next target: the Merchants Association. Not only had it failed to call on members to desegregate, but it also led the campaign against the public accommodations ordinance. And now it was telling the COB to fold up its tent and go home. Quinton Baker planned a sit-in, with Pat Cusick in charge.

On July 19, 1963, Pat and about twenty other young volunteers walked into the Merchants Association building on West Franklin Street and sat down on the lobby floor. Locking arms, they sang, "Oh, Freedom":

No more Jim Crow, no more Jim Crow,
No more Jim Crow over me.
And before I'll be a slave,
I'll be buried in my grave,
And go home to my Lord and be free.

The Merchants Association's manager, Joe Augustine, stepped from his office. "Mr. Cusick," he said, "you can stay in here all day so far as I'm concerned if you'll just stop singing. We can't do our work." As the singing continued, the police walked in. Augustine borrowed their bullhorn, telling the protesters he'd give them thirty seconds to stop. They didn't. The police carried them out past a crush of reporters, photographers and television cameramen. A COB member who witnessed the event from across the street said:

> *The police must have been waiting for just this chance. They stacked the limp bodies up at the curb, which was completely unnecessary. They did it because they were out for Cusick. They believed Cusick had started all this and they knew he had trained these young people, so they stacked the bodies up on the sidewalk on top of Cusick. They laid them out just like you lay out dead bodies....I hadn't seen anything like it since I was in [the war in] Korea.*
>
> *As the police cars arrived, they would pull bodies off, drag them along the street, throw them into the police cars. It was so bad that the other people there, the children and other ones who hadn't been scheduled to be arrested, sat down on the sidewalk in protest. So they were arrested. They went limp, as they were trained to do, and the cars came and carried them off, too.*

In all, the police carried off twenty-seven Black and seven white protestors, including Harold Foster and Pat Cusick.

The *Weekly* harshly condemned the demonstration. Chapel Hill was bitterly divided, putting its reputation as a southern paradise under threat. The vast majority of whites—even many so-called liberals—demanded an end to direct action.

Cracks formed in the COB organization. Its white liberals and Black youth were locked in a power struggle over strategy. In August 1963, the group split. Demoralized, Harold Foster decided to take a break from activism and focus on his education.

Meanwhile, another organization took the baton. With help from Black Durham attorney and civil rights activist Floyd McKissick, local Black youths and their white university allies formed a chapter of the Congress of Racial Equality (CORE). John Dunne surrendered his scholarship at UNC to work full-time as CORE's director for twenty-five dollars a week. The "Negro cause" had become his own. Pat Cusick and Quinton Baker lent their advice.

On July 19, 1963, protesters were arrested and stacked up "like cordwood" on West Franklin Street awaiting patrol cars. *Jim Wallace Photographic Collection, University Libraries, University of North Carolina at Chapel Hill.*

On December 12, 1963, four of the Merchants Association demonstrators were convicted of trespassing. Pat Cusick and three women were sentenced to thirty days in jail or a fifty-dollar fine plus court costs. In response, they issued this statement: "We will not pay fines for our protest for freedom and human dignity. We will not contribute money to support an institution that supports racial injustice. The conscience of the community and the nation must be awakened to the task of eliminating segregation. This is best done through individual sacrifice."

Pat thought they would shake the hearts and minds of Chapel Hill by voluntarily serving thirty days in jail rather than paying a fine. "We couldn't have been more mistaken," he later admitted. "They were glad we were put away." Pat was sentenced to thirty days on the Durham County chain gang.

The prison sentences and the community's response gave rise to another action group. The Chapel Hill Freedom Committee was a consortium of area civil rights organizations. John Dunne and Quinton Baker served as co-chairmen. Raising the stakes, they planned a rash of shocking demonstrations at segregated restaurants.

On December 13, they staged a sit-in at the Pines Restaurant. The participants were David Dansby, head of the campus chapter of the NAACP; Phyllis Timberlake, a young Black woman; David McReynolds, a leading white liberal visiting town for speaking engagements; and John Dunne. McReynolds described the event:

We drove out to the Pines, Chapel Hill's only elegant eatery, and walked in. The hostess dashed over as soon as we got in the door and asked us to leave. Dunne didn't refuse, but he didn't leave. The manager, a Mr. Leroy Merritt, came on the scene. He exploded almost immediately: "We're segregated! Everybody in Chapel Hill knows we're segregated! You got to leave right now!" Dunne spoke quietly about how he had made a reservation by phone and hadn't been told Negroes wouldn't be served, and, pointing to me, said I was a visiting speaker and he had planned to have me out for dinner at the best place in town, and now he was terribly embarrassed, etc.

All this time the moral elite of Chapel Hill continued to come into the restaurant, walk by, and sit down to their dinners. And all this time Mr. Leroy Merritt got redder in the face and kept yelling, "You gotta get out of here!" Then he called the police. They arrived almost at once, with poor Mr. Leroy by now almost inarticulate and on the verge of apoplexy.... The four of us were ushered out and, to our dismay, notified we would be arrested as soon as Mr. Leroy Merritt could get down to the station to sign the warrants.

John Carswell and son forcefully remove Lincoln High School student James Brittain from Colonial Drug, December 1963. *Photo by Al Amon. John Ehle Papers #4555, Southern Historical Collection, Wilson Library, University of North Carolina at Chapel Hill.*

Sit-in at Brady's Restaurant on East Franklin Street, December 1963. On the site today is the Siena Hotel. *Jim Wallace Photographic Collection, University Libraries, University of North Carolina at Chapel Hill.*

Over the next couple of weeks, activists staged sit-ins at Brady's Restaurant, Leo's Restaurant, Clarence's Bar and Grill and a beer hall called the Shack. At the Tar Heel Sandwich Shop, one of the Black protesters got kicked in the head. Activists also returned to their old standby, Colonial Drug. Again, none of the segregated businesses gave an inch.

CORE ATTEMPTED TO CAPITALIZE on holiday cheer and goodwill. On December 15, seventy demonstrators marched silently through town, carrying signs reading, "Give Freedom for Christmas." John Dunne issued an official statement, calling for a public accommodations ordinance before Christmas. It didn't happen. On Christmas Day, he and Quinton held CORE staff meetings. They also visited the local jail, bringing a pineapple cake Quinton had baked. Perhaps it would comfort the eleven demonstrators spending Christmas behind bars.

Four days later, in an attempt to bridge the public divide, a panel discussion between town leaders and protest organizers was held at the Chapel of the Cross. John and Quinton served as panelists, along with Mayor McClamroch, Alderman Giduz, Police Chief Blake and Joe Augustine. About 250 townspeople attended. During the tense discussion, Quinton defended the protests: "Is it not the American tradition that when a law is being used unjustly, you make the most effective protest you can?" For his part, Alderman Giduz announced he would be ready to vote on the public accommodations ordinance at the Board of Aldermen's January meeting. Would he break the logjam?

THE ACTIVISTS WERE IN serious danger, and not just because the local media had stirred up anger toward them. They had publicly vowed not to fight back against assailants or bring charges against them. It was open season on protesters. Regardless, many of them were prepared to make the ultimate sacrifice for the sake of human rights and justice.

On the evening of New Year's Day 1964, John, Quinton and four other protesters entered a segregated grocery store at East Franklin Street and Estes Drive, Carlton's Rock Pile (it was built with stone). Quinton picked up a box of cookies and told owner Carlton Mize he'd like to buy them. "I don't serve niggers," Mize snapped, "and that goes for white niggers, too, so all of you get out of here." The protesters sat down on the floor. Mize grabbed a mop, dipped it in bleach and ammonia and squeezed it on the demonstrators' heads. Three of them, coughing and gagging, managed to escape. Left behind were John, Quinton and white UNC student Lou Calhoun. As Quinton and Lou came up for air, they got smacked across the face by the wet mop. John saw Mize tilt Quinton's head back and pour ammonia straight from a bottle into his mouth. Somehow, Quinton and Lou stumbled to the door and got out. Mize poured ammonia over John's entire body, even under his waistband, until his skin was burning. As Mize reached behind the counter for a baseball bat, John thought his life was over. But at that very moment, Police Chief Blake burst into the store. All of the demonstrators were taken to the hospital. Quinton had his stomach pumped, and John was treated for second-degree burns. All six were arrested for trespassing.

Another shocking incident took place the next day. Lou Calhoun and two Black high school girls entered Watts Restaurant on 15-501 just south of town, operated by Austin and Jeppie Watts. A "very heavy woman," Jeppie demanded that the activists leave. They didn't. Jeppie began kicking Lou, so he balled up on the floor. Then Jeppie stood over him, hiked up her skirt, squatted and urinated on his head. The customers applauded her. Police arrived and arrested all the demonstrators.

The next night, January 3, the Freedom Committee sent eleven activists back to Watts Restaurant. They included John, Quinton and several

A stronghold of segregation, Watts Restaurant stood across 15-501 from today's Southern Village. *Roland Giduz Photographic Collection #P0033, North Carolina Collection Photographic Archives, Louis Round Wilson Special Collections Library, University of North Carolina at Chapel Hill.*

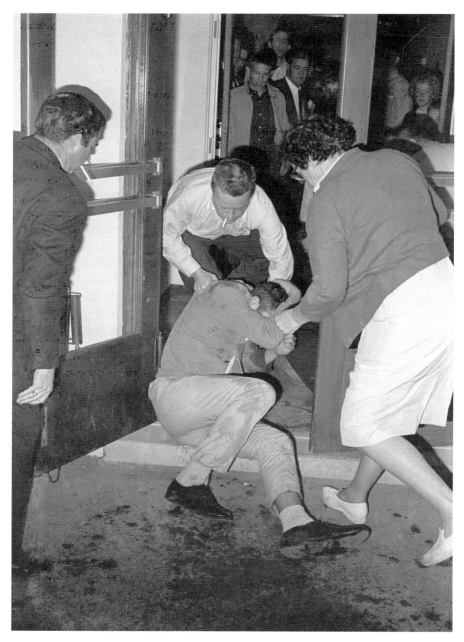

During a sit-in at Watts Restaurant on January 3, 1964, UNC psychology professor Al Amon was seriously injured. *Jim Wallace Photographic Collection, University Libraries, University of North Carolina at Chapel Hill.*

professors from UNC and Duke. Perhaps the professors would command a measure of respect. Before entering the establishment, the activists were "jumped on in the parking lot and beaten." But they were undeterred. When they got to the entrance, UNC professor Al Amon asked if they could be served. Recognizing him from the day before, Austin Watts yanked him into the foyer and knocked him to the floor. Watts and another employee kicked him repeatedly, leaving a gash on the back of his head. He blacked out. Serving as shields, John and Quinton threw themselves on top of him while Jeppie Watts beat all three with a broom handle. The customers yelled things like, "Kill them, get the professors!" The three protesters were thrown out into the cold and sprayed in the face with a garden hose, making it difficult to breathe. An employee yelled an obscenity, suggesting where the hose should be shoved. Finally, the police showed up, and Amon was taken to the emergency room.

Over the next week or so, sit-ins were held at Watts Restaurant, Brady's Restaurant, Leo's Restaurant, Clarence's Grill, the Tar Heel Sandwich Shop, Colonial Drug and Fowler's grocery store. Again, none of the segregated businesses gave an inch.

The Freedom Committee decided to temporarily call off protests pending the second vote on the public accommodations ordinance. Pat Cusick was released from prison on January 5, 1964, allowing him to be in Chapel Hill for the showdown.

On January 12, the eve of the big vote, the Freedom Committee held its "Walk for Freedom" from the western part of Durham to the outskirts of Chapel Hill. As sleet and freezing rain fell, 170 demonstrators participated. Joined by about 175 Chapel Hillians gathered at Eastgate Shopping Center, the entire group walked the final mile together to a mass meeting at First Baptist Church. After passing "such citadels of segregation" as Brady's, Carlton's Rock Pile and the Frozen Kustard without incident, the marchers were hurled with epithets and "scattered obscenities" by students at the Alpha Tau Omega fraternity house, reported the *Tar Heel*. Another incident "almost led to blows when a man who identified himself as the Grand Dragon of the North Carolina Ku Klux Klan threatened to assault a cameraman who took his picture."

Culminating the march, at least five hundred people packed into First Baptist Church on Roberson Street for speeches from civil rights activist Floyd McKissick and author John Knowles. Speaking last was CORE leader James Farmer. "Chapel Hill is a key to the South and the nation," he declared. The room thundered with applause. Marking the fourth

On January 12, 1964, the Walk for Freedom rallied support for the Public Accommodations Ordinance. *Jim Wallace Photographic Collection, University Libraries, University of North Carolina at Chapel Hill.*

anniversary of the Greensboro sit-in, Farmer announced a deadline for the town to pass the languishing ordinance. "Unless Chapel Hill is an open city by February 1," he warned, "it will become the focal point of all our efforts. All our resources—staff, funds and training—will be centered here."

MANY WHITE TOWNSPEOPLE COULDN'T understand why civil rights activists were so worked up about Chapel Hill, of all places. It was more progressive than most southern cities, right? In the summer of 1963, the Merchants Association estimated that 90 to 95 percent of local businesses were integrated, a figure that was "bandied about" and accepted as fact for months. But it was based on a junk survey. The association had studied about 250 *retail establishments* rather than *places of public accommodation*—and hadn't even called all of them. So, in January 1964, the *Daily Tar Heel* polled businesses falling closely under the category of public accommodation. To their surprise, they found that a full 25 percent of them "practiced some form of discrimination in service to Negroes." Even more telling, 32 percent of the restaurants discriminated in some way, whether serving Negroes only at the back door or the stand-up counter or refusing service entirely. Five of the nine establishments listed as serving beer or ale didn't offer equal service, translating to a full 55 percent discrimination. "Despite what you hear to the contrary," the paper concluded, "racial discrimination here is far from being a straw man." But the general public continued to live in an alternate universe, since the *Tar Heel* was circulated only among the campus population. Perhaps the protests would have gained more support if the truth had been known all along.

ON THE EVENING OF January 13, 1964—climaxing a month of demonstrations with some 239 arrests—the Board of Aldermen met for the second vote on the public accommodations ordinance. The room was packed. The initial discussion centered on a report from UNC's Institute of Government prepared by professor George H. Esser Jr. that addressed the legal aspects of the proposed law. Esser noted that the legality of such a law was unknown and that there was little precedent for it. His report asserted that "no one can advise you with any degree of legal certainty what the Supreme Court of North Carolina would rule in such a situation." After a ninety-minute debate, the board took a vote. It mirrored their first one, four to two. Standing outside Town Hall, Pat Cusick got the news. Heaving a sigh, he sank down to the ice-cold concrete.

The next morning, at a press conference in Durham, James Farmer stepped before the cameras. "We mean business," he remarked, repeating his ultimatum that Chapel Hill be fully integrated by February 1 or face the consequences. While the Board of Aldermen refused to be intimidated, the activists were as determined as ever. The nation watched and waited.

Bracing for the worst, Police Chief Blake brought in reinforcements. On the morning of February 1, officers from the sheriff's department and a contingent of highway patrolmen rolled into town. Joining the mix were fifteen officers from the Burlington Police Department wearing riot helmets.

As promised, the day was filled with shock-and-awe demonstrations. As 350 activists marched from St. Joseph's Church to Town Hall for a rally, a few of them sat with picket signs in a crosswalk on Franklin Street. Police loaded twenty-two protestors into the new paddy wagon—a converted milk truck—and took them to the town jail.

Earlier, as the marchers passed the bus station, violence erupted. "Two or three white men went into the Western Auto Store across the street and picked up shovels," Chief Blake recalled. "They came outside and one of them began to hit every Negro he could get to before we arrested him." That evening, fifty-three demonstrators were arrested during sit-ins at Brady's Restaurant and Carlton's Rock Pile. Once again, none of the segregated businesses gave an inch. The activists hadn't won a single victory for seven months.

QUINTON BELIEVED THAT CREATING havoc gave activists political power. It forced the public to face an issue. On Saturday, February 8, 1964, the day of the big UNC–Wake Forest basketball game, his most ambitious plan to date threw Chapel Hill into utter chaos. At 1:45 that afternoon, Floyd McKissick led a march of about 350 people from a Black church down Franklin Street and back again. Then, about 150 of them—those willing to be arrested—remained for a second wave of action. At 3:30 p.m., about 110 people marched to the corner of Franklin and Columbia Streets and "walked in a large S into the middle of the intersection." They sat down, blocking traffic. A large crowd of whites on the sidewalk yelled at them.

At that same moment, the other demonstrators blocked the four highways leading out of town. Just west of Eastgate Shopping Center, three Blacks and two whites sat down on Durham Road (East Franklin Street). A driver inched forward until his bumper touched two prone demonstrators. In no time, traffic was backed up half a mile in both directions.

Meanwhile, eleven demonstrators blocked the road to Pittsboro (South Columbia Street), near 15-501. Angry white men from Merritt's gas station (now Merritt's Grill) yanked the demonstrators off the road, but they jumped right back on. Their clothing was torn, signs were ripped from their hands and two or three of them were beaten and tossed into the bushes along the curb. As police arrived on the scene, the white men attacked a television cameraman from Charlotte.

Demonstrators also blocked Raleigh Road where it intersected Country Club Road. Campus police dragged seven of them off the street, but they returned and sat down again. Just before the basketball game let out, they headed to Woollen Gymnasium to block the parking lot exits. The campus police dragged them out of the way. Only a few cars could get through before the demonstrators crawled back. Demonstrators also "seized the floor" of the basketball game.

Meanwhile, at the intersection of Franklin and Columbia Streets, Chief Blake had finally managed to get the huge crowd out of the road. But before long, eight demonstrators came back and lay down. Speeding cars weaved in and out between them.

That night, about sixty demonstrators returned to the intersection and lay down on the pavement. A woman drove her car up to one of them until one of her tires touched him. He refused to budge. In all, ninety-eight people were arrested that day. The public divide was deeper than ever.

On February 8, 1964, sit-ins again blocked traffic on Franklin Street. *Jim Wallace Photographic Collection, University Libraries, University of North Carolina at Chapel Hill.*

The following Monday night, February 10, protesters again blocked the main intersection of town. As police carried about fifty of them into Town Hall, John and Pat watched helplessly at the door. John heard that the Board of Aldermen was in session upstairs discussing mundane parking matters instead of the racial crisis. Suddenly, he felt every ounce of energy drain from his soul. It seemed the town was determined to turn a deaf ear to his cause. He faced facts. He could no longer put the lives of fellow activists at risk. What he needed was an entirely new tack.

AT SUNRISE ON PALM Sunday, March 22, 1964, John and three other activists gathered on a small patch of grass in front of the post office on East Franklin Street. They were commencing an eight-day fast. (Dr. King had talked them out of going all the way and dying.) John was joined by Pat Cusick, Black high school student James Foushee and Reverend LaVert Taylor, who served on Dr. King's staff. They had mimeographed a leaflet to explain the demonstration:

> *Holy Week Fast*
> *Beginning Palm Sunday, and continuing through Easter Sunday, several persons will participate in a Holy Week fast. The participants will remain in front of the Post Office and will take only water for the eight-day period. The fast is in keeping with the philosophy of Satyagraha (nonviolence) advocated by M.K. Gandhi….Our fast calls to attention the daily sufferings of the Negro citizens of Chapel Hill….*
>
> *We believe that a fast is the highest form of prayer, and look upon this Holy Week fast as a prayer that the city will live up to its responsibilities—and of course the "city" is not a vague and abstract concept; it is the duly elected officials and each person who resides in Chapel Hill. We hope that by fasting publicly, we can remind each person that we have not solved this problem and we hope that each of us, as we observe the final week of Lent, will ask ourselves the question, "Have I honestly and sincerely done all in my power to eliminate racial discrimination in Chapel Hill?"*

At first, there was some heckling and name-calling. But as Holy Week ticked by, some white liberals dropped by to offer support. John told a *Daily Tar Heel* reporter that "the incidents of kindness have far outnumbered the incidents of name-calling….People have stopped to talk to us and encourage us. Some brought cigarettes, blankets, and other items. One lady brought us a vase of flowers."

Holy Week Fast, 1964. *Left to right*: Pat Cusick, Reverend LaVert Taylor, John Dunne and high school student James Foushee. *Photo by Al Amon. John Ehle Papers #4555, Southern Historical Collection, Wilson Library, University of North Carolina at Chapel Hill.*

That Saturday evening, however, the feel-good atmosphere evaporated. "The Klan passed through in a cavalcade of cars with their hated white robes, masks, and guns," Pat recalled. Later that night, the KKK held a rally in a field on 15-501, three miles northeast of town. A twenty-five-foot cross burned as a crowd of about seven hundred people stood by. Speaking from the back of a flatbed truck under the glare of television lights, Georgia Klan official Calvin Craig lambasted Chapel Hill post office officials for allowing the fasters to "loiter" on the city's post office lawn. He predicted that the federal civil rights bill then before Congress would spark massive bloodshed across America, whether it passed or not. A North Carolina Klan official voiced hope that the next governor would be a "states' rights" man.

Following the rally, the Klansmen dined at Watts Restaurant. After dessert and coffee, some of them showed up outside the post office to confront the fasters and their supporters. Although "several scuffles broke out," the violence could have been far worse if police hadn't been on hand. Originally, the Klan planned to kill the fasters with a drum of sulfuric acid. But the

Klan's Orange County branch, fearing they'd bear the brunt of the blame, had the plot scrapped.

On Easter Sunday, the day after the Klan rally, the Holy Week fast broke. As John stood up, a crisply dressed little Black boy walked up to him. John picked him up in his arms and smiled down at him. An eyewitness said, "It made a beautiful picture." Unfortunately, however, the fast was of no benefit whatsoever to the freedom movement.

In late April 1964, the law finally caught up with John, Quinton and Pat. They pleaded no contest to their roles in the February street-blocking demonstrations. With public contempt for their movement—and their leadership roles in it—Superior Court judge Raymond Mallard slapped them with harsh sentences. He called them communists.

Pat was sentenced to twelve months of hard labor on the state roads for obstructing traffic and to two years of the same for resisting arrest. (The judge ruled that "going limp" constituted resisting arrest, even though there was no precedent.) Pat's two-year sentence was suspended for five years.

John was sentenced to twelve months in jail for obstructing traffic and to two years in jail for resisting arrest. The latter sentence was suspended for five years.

Quinton was sentenced to six months in jail, payment of court costs and a $150 fine. He was also ordered to return under $1,000 bond in August for sentencing on a second count.

The judge had effectively taken the movement's leaders out of circulation. A *Daily Tar Heel* editorial stated, "Judge Mallard has accomplished his purpose—to destroy the civil rights movement in Chapel Hill—and he has gone to every extent to do so."

After John was taken back to his holding cell in chains, he wrote a letter to his parents on a long strip of toilet paper that he later smuggled out. In part, it read:

> *Dearest Folks:*
> *Well, here we are!! In February, 117 Americans made a protest and in doing so chose to disobey the laws. Now, as responsible citizens we are paying the legitimate cost of that action....The source of my sorrow is the cruel lie which this court and the system it serves continues to perpetrate upon the unfortunate masses of white people: as long as the white people of this country are allowed to believe that this revolution is anything but a*

result of the legitimate anger and frustration of the oppressed people of this country, violence and tragedy will continue to grow. Judge Mallard bears great responsibility for everyone who dies or is hurt in the coming months of racial violence—for everyone whose soul is further frozen with hatred…he spoke in the incredibly ignorant and guilt-ridden words of the Klan, that we are all pawns or malicious agents of "the international conspiracy," that we were all paid $6.00 a day by Northern funds to come into the South, warping young people's minds to think that Christianity permits you to break the law with impunity, that we were all alien forces of an alien power being supported by alien funds, and so on and on. I am afraid—afraid that I will be forced to see the disintegration of America and the dream it once symbolized, the light it once gave the world.

On July 2, 1964, as John, Quinton and Pat languished in jail, President Lyndon Johnson signed the Civil Rights Act. A watershed piece of legislation, it prohibited discrimination in public accommodations nationwide. The Chapel Hill activists may have thought they had nothing to do with it. Yet, combined with thousands of demonstrators across the country, their pressure campaign is what got Congress to act.

Local students decided to "test" the new law's effectiveness. On the night of July 3, a small group of Blacks and whites entered Brady's Restaurant. They were served without incident. But then they went to Watts Restaurant. Austin Watts stood in the doorway, refusing them entry. Within moments, about eight people burst from the restaurant, "swinging clubs and fists." A few days later, activists reported that local businesses were in full compliance.

In August 1964, John, Quinton and Pat were paroled and exiled. John and Quinton received scholarships, John from Harvard and Quinton from the University of Wisconsin. Pat went to Boston to work in a poverty program.

Of course, we can't forget Harold Foster—one of the Chapel Hill Nine—for bravely leading the desegregation battle in its first three years. Recruited by Black newspapers in New York, he joined a new movement for racial pride and self-determination. He returned to Chapel Hill in 1978 to help his ailing mother. In 2017, at the age of seventy-five, he died at a Pittsboro nursing home.

The Chapel Hill Nine Monument at 450 West Franklin Street, designed by Durham artist Stephen Hayes. *Photo by author.*

ON THE AFTERNOON OF February 28, 2020—the sixtieth anniversary of the Chapel Hill Nine's first sit-in at Colonial Drug—a crowd gathered where the store once stood at 450 West Franklin Street. A marker was unveiled to commemorate the historic civil rights event. Those present included the four surviving members of the Chapel Hill Nine: Douglas "Clyde" Perry, James Merritt, Albert Williams and David Mason Jr. One of the speakers at the ceremony was Harold Foster's sister Esphur. She admitted that the work he sparked was far from over. "We remind you," she said, "that the tussle continues."

7

THE ROOM 201 MYSTERY

Officials speculated that something occurred between 9:30 and 11 p.m.
that played a part in the tragedy.
—Evening Star *(Washington, D.C.), October 8, 1961*

F riday, October 6, 1961, was a haunting day for Cobb Dorm janitor Robert Holt. At the time, the UNC residence hall was male-only.

Around ten o'clock that morning, according to routine, Holt entered a room on the second floor. He was surprised to find the two roommates still in bed, seemingly asleep, but thought little of it. He swept the floor and moved on.

An hour later, he received a call from Lenoir Dining Hall. Why hadn't the two boys reported for work? Holt returned to the room for another look. This time, he realized that both boys were dead.

A barrage of police and university officials arrived on the scene. Bill Johnson and Mike Barham were lying on their backs in "unnaturally straight" positions, dressed in pajamas. A pillow completely covered Johnson's face, and a blanket nearly covered Barham's. The bodies were removed amid a crowd of photographers and gawkers.

Prompt autopsies revealed that the boys died of cyanide poisoning. Milkshake cups and crackers in their room were tested for cyanide but came up negative. With no clues to go on, Police Chief William Blake told the *Weekly*, "We're trying to find out how the poison was administered and by whom." The North Carolina State Bureau of Investigation was called in to verify the cyanide tests.

Naturally, students and townspeople were spooked. Chief Blake assured them there was no cause for concern: "We don't think anyone's going around poisoning people." Newspapers carried the sensational story in cities and towns throughout the eastern United States.

Although the boys had been close, they were polar opposites. Barham, twenty, was handsome, outgoing and friendly, with close-cropped blond hair and a cleft chin. A pre-med student, he played trumpet for the University Band and a small dance combo. Johnson, twenty-four, was a graduate student in industrial relations. With a dark face, deep-set eyes and dark-rimmed glasses, he was introverted and rarely smiled.

Reportedly, the University Band was reluctant to perform at the football game the day after the bodies were found, since Barham was absent from its ranks. It was also said that the Carolina football players, who gave a lackluster performance in their loss against Clemson, had been affected by the tragedy.

The two boys had worked together the previous summer in a Greensboro restaurant, sharing a room in a boardinghouse. The restaurant owner described them as "extremely fond of each other." Barham dated a girl or two while working in Greensboro, but Johnson apparently did not.

A few days after classes started at UNC that September, Johnson went to extraordinary lengths to have his room switched so he could live with Barham. Johnson also got a job at Lenoir Hall so they could work together again. This struck some as odd, since Johnson wore expensive clothes, drove a late-model car and always seemed to have lots of money. Their beds had matching spreads, and their window was decorated with green plaid drapes. Setting them apart even more from other students, the pair had a television set and kept their room as neat as a pin.

Investigators interviewed dozens of students, trying to trace the boys' movements the day before they were found dead. Barham's whereabouts for most of the day were known, but Johnson's activities from about 9:30 to 11:00 p.m. were not. Barham had been seen in a downtown pool room between 9:00 and 9:30 p.m. and in his dorm room shortly afterward. Then, around 11:00 p.m., he burst from the room and staggered to the bathroom. He began retching, collapsed unconscious on the tile floor and went into convulsions. Another student ran from the bathroom to alert Johnson. "Barham's sick," the student blurted. "Is he drunk?"

"He doesn't drink," Johnson replied.

Several students helped Barham up and carried him back toward his room. As they fumbled down the hall, Johnson muttered that Barham was drunk again, contradicting what he had said moments earlier. As they laid

Barham on a bed in his room—apparently still unconscious—one student suggested calling an ambulance. Johnson didn't seem concerned. Neither Barham nor Johnson were seen alive again.

Four days after the boys were found dead, police got an important clue. A chemistry student disclosed that Johnson had been asking around for a "fast-acting poison." It was strong circumstantial evidence. Chief Blake gave an update on the case, saying, "It was either murder-suicide, double murder, or a suicide pact."

According to rumor on campus, Johnson was upset at Barham's sudden "indifference" to him. Rejection can be a powerful motive for murder. So can jealousy. It was said that Barham was supposed to have had a date with a girl in Greensboro on the sixth. Did Johnson want more than friendship from Barham but got rebuffed?

There was no proof as to where the cyanide was obtained or how it was administered. But late that month, police hypothesized that the two students died from powdered cyanide sprinkled on crackers during a card game the final night.

Amateur sleuths tried to help the police fill in the blanks. A grad student at Princeton University asserted that a "nationwide underworld organization" had been operating in Chapel Hill. In similar tones, a woman dialed Chief Blake long distance to say the deaths were tied to a "big dope ring." A woman in Jasper, Alabama, wrote Blake a four-page letter in red ink that read, "This sounds like the art of a magic cult that has been operating in this area since 1861." Although the police chief always welcomed tips from the public, he likely laughed these off.

In early January 1962, after receiving a final report from the Chapel Hill Police Department on the bizarre case, the North Carolina State Bureau of Investigation issued a formal statement. The boys died "as a result of the act of one or both of them," said District Solicitor Ike Andrews. There was no evidence that a third party was involved. It seemed likely that many facts would never be known and that no one would ever be charged.

In the fall of 1962, turning the page on the episode, university officials switched Cobb to a women-only dorm. But that wasn't forever, either.

8

THE SPEAKER BAN LAW

Vestige of the Red Scare

*Communist strategists play upon young,
immature minds as a maestro plays a violin.*
—*Jesse Helms, July 9, 1963*

W hen civil rights protests rocked the South in the spring of 1963, many blamed a rising tide of communist infiltration. The loudest voice was probably right-winger Jesse Helms, who attacked UNC–Chapel Hill in his fiery television editorials from WRAL-TV in Raleigh. In April 1963, he called on the university's administration to investigate communist activity on campus.

Later that spring, Helms upped the ante. He praised a bill in Ohio that restricted radical figures from speaking at publicly funded colleges. Conservatives in the North Carolina legislature were listening.

Just four days later, in the waning hours of the 1963 session of the North Carolina General Assembly, conservatives rammed through House Bill 1395, "An Act to Regulate Visiting Speakers." Modeled after Ohio's similar bill, it banned speeches at North Carolina's public universities by "known" members of the Communist Party; persons "known" to support the overthrow of the constitutions of North Carolina or the United States; or anyone who had invoked the Fifth Amendment in congressional investigations about subversive activities. Also passing in the state senate, the "Speaker Ban" became law.

As if the civil rights protests hadn't riled up Chapel Hill enough, the Speaker Ban—dubbed the "gag law"—threw the town into a tizzy.

Louis Graves, editor of the *Chapel Hill Weekly*, insisted that the law was a "total fraud." He saw it as payback for UNC's failure to restrain civil rights demonstrators. "The gag law is the University's comeuppance for harboring liberals, integrationists, and a spirit of true freedom," he wrote.

Blindsided by the new law, UNC officials roundly repudiated it. In a joint statement, President Bill Friday and Chancellor William B. Aycock said, "We shall request the Board of Trustees to seek repeal of this legislation.... This limitation on the free flow of ideas on campuses is both unnecessary and injurious."

UNC's Faculty Council also took a stand, unanimously passing a resolution against the Speaker Ban. It called into question its constitutionality and its harm to the university's academic mission.

On July 9, 1963, Jesse Helms went on television again, responding to UNC's objections. He said, in part:

> *Academic freedom is not involved here, unless one has peculiar ideas of what and how students are to be taught. Freedom of speech is not involved. Communists and Fifth-Amendment fellow travelers still have the right to speak. The people, through their elected legislators, have simply said that those who seek to undermine and destroy our country must henceforth find their own forum. And those who wish to hear them must henceforth do so in the full knowledge that they are listening to deliberate, calculating enemies of America.*
>
> *It is merely a question of whether communists and those sympathetic to communism shall be tagged for what they are. Up to now, they have slipped upon our campuses under the guise of entertainers, or as citizens with "a different kind of political philosophy." It is fair to say that they have found their forums comfortable and receptive in an atmosphere of so-called liberalism.*

Other supporters of the ban included local judge Luther J. Phipps, the American Legion, the John Birch Society and those whom one Chapel Hillian called "the Jesse Helms anti-everything kind."

Local playwright and liberal activist Paul Green publicly criticized the Speaker Ban. In mid-October 1963, in a University Day address at Hill Hall, he called it "an error in law-making." As reported in the *Chapel Hill Weekly*, he added:

How can the students have a chance to know the truth, to examine and see the world as it really is if they are to be denied the chance to hear points of view from all sides?

A great many of the legislators who voted for this bill were graduates of this University....But what did they do really? They didn't hurt the communists, say, but they did hurt the university....

I am not afraid of communists coming to lecture on this campus. I think they should. We need a chance to hear the Marxists talk, hear the communists speak out their palaver. That is a good way in pointing out the errors of Marxism, of finding what it's all about. Thus our students can develop their own strength and belief in our own democracy. Anyone knows that the way to weaken a child is to shelter it too much. It must have exercise, stretch its muscles, and its mind also must have exercise. A great disservice then was done to us when this bill was passed.

Helms went right back on television and delivered a scathing attack on Green, saying he had "merely pulled the trigger on an overworked pop-gun." After spending most of his rant linking Green to communists and liberals, Helms did his best to paint him as an irrelevant, washed-up writer.

Green wrote a friend that "hedge priest Jesse" was a threat to democracy, adding, "We must work in charity and dedication to make it survive." He was invited to appear on television but surmised that "the next evening and all the evenings thereafter good old Jesse would be in there whaling the lard out of me and whooping it up for his cause."

In late October 1963, UNC's Board of Trustees resolved to support the repeal or amendment of the Speaker Ban. It recommended the creation of a special committee, appointed by Democratic governor Terry Sanford, to seek changes in the law.

Due to politics, however, Governor Sanford denied the request for a full year. In October 1964, in the final days of his administration, he finally appointed a committee, comprising members of the Board of Trustees, to make a "careful, full and detailed study" of the Speaker Ban Law.

The committee presented its report to the new governor, Dan K. Moore, in January 1965. It recommended transferring control and authority over speakers to university trustees. But Governor Moore didn't support efforts to amend the law during the 1965 legislative session. The controversy dragged on.

THAT MAY, UNIVERSITY OFFICIALS got more bad news. The Southern Association of Colleges and Schools threatened UNC's accreditation status. After all, the Speaker Ban restricted "academic freedom" and prevented the Board of Trustees from running the university without political interference.

If UNC was to lack accreditation, it wouldn't be able to compete in college athletics. Apathy swiftly gave way to panic and action, said law professor Daniel Pollitt, since the university might not be able to "compete in the athletic field and we would not get grants and all that."

For his part, Paul Green delivered his message to the state at large, penning a lengthy editorial in Raleigh's *News & Observer*. Declaring himself "an ardent believer in democracy," he said, in part:

> Ours is a doctrine and a practice of freedom.... The free and active mind is the one certain and sure defense against an ever-threatening barbarism. When this goes down, the citadel of glory falls and the funeral pall of omnipotent death eclipses the guiding light.... The teachers and scholars of our universities and colleges are in a special sense the keepers of this light. And as such they must have free play for their intelligence and imagination....If totalitarian philosophy is at variance with the true doctrine of democracy, and I believe it is, whether of communism or fascism, then the means our educational institutions have to combat it is not by fiat or decree but by a more zealous devotion to and spreading of the truth.... The tradition of freedom of conscience and individual rights has long been established among us... The Speaker Ban Law was and is an asinine piece of legislation. It is a disgrace to North Carolina. It should be abolished, and the quicker the better. Let the legislators now assembled in Raleigh, I say, boldly and sensibly face up to this matter.

ON JUNE 1, 1965, Governor Moore recommended that a commission be formed to examine the law and suggest remedies to the legislature. Following the Britt Commission's televised public hearings that August and September, a compromise bill returned control over speakers to campus trustees—but under strict guidelines.

Student leaders at UNC flatly opposed the compromise. They insisted that there should be no restrictions on speakers whatsoever.

Things heated up even more when the Students for a Democratic Society (SDS) invited Frank Wilkinson, who had pleaded the Fifth on whether he was a communist, and Herbert Aptheker, a member of the Communist Party

USA, to speak at UNC to challenge the law. While the Board of Trustees waffled on the idea, acting chancellor J. Carlyle Sitterson used his authority to nix the plan.

Student body president Paul Dickson III, a twenty-four-year-old veteran, didn't take the decision sitting down. He secretly met with President Friday to discuss strategy for a federal court challenge. In a calculated move, Dickson arranged for Frank Wilkinson to speak on campus the following spring. The trap was set.

TENSIONS RAN HIGH WHEN Wilkinson arrived in Chapel Hill on March 2, 1966. According to plan, Dickson and other student organizers ushered him onto the campus lawn at McCorkle Place. UNC's police chief arrived on the scene and forbade Wilkinson from speaking. The students turned,

Paul Dickson III introduces Frank Wilkinson to about 1,200 students on the campus side of a rock wall. *Photo by Jock Lauterer. University of North Carolina at Chapel Hill Library Photographic Services Copy Negatives #P0086, North Carolina Collection Photographic Archives, Wilson Library, University of North Carolina at Chapel Hill.*

Paul Dickson III was instrumental in overturning the Speaker Ban Law. *Jock Lauterer Photographic Collection #P0069, North Carolina Collection Photographic Archives, Wilson Library, University of North Carolina at Chapel Hill.*

leading Wilkinson to a sidewalk just across the campus line. Addressing a sprawling crowd of UNC students, he said in part, "I am interested in my Constitutional right to speak, but I am equally concerned or even more concerned with your right to hear....I refuse to stand on a sidewalk at a wall of this great University and try to shout over this wall to reach you with the message which I have. It is an important message."

A week later, on March 9, the students went through the whole charade again with Herbert Aptheker. When the campus police chief told Aptheker he couldn't speak, Dickson had all the legal ammo he needed to file the suit.

ALMOST TWO FULL YEARS later, on February 19, 1968, a three-judge federal district court in Greensboro ruled that the Speaker Ban Law was unconstitutional and violated First Amendment protections of free speech. In a joint statement, President Friday and Chancellor Sitterson said they hoped the decision brought "this long and costly controversy to an end." No appeal was filed.

But the episode did have a curious postscript. In 1979, when Jesse Helms was one of Paul Green's senators, Green wrote him, deeply concerned about the nuclear arms race. Now *this* was one issue they could both get behind. They declared a truce of sorts. In the spring of 1980, Green invited Helms to his farm in Chatham County for a chat under the shade of maple trees. "Oh, I've looked forward to this for a long time," the practiced politician gushed. "You've always been one of my favorite people."

9

THE *CHAPEL HILL WEEKLY*

Homespun News

*R.E. Coker, the zoologist, called up Monday night,
said that he had a live loon at his house.*
—Chapel Hill Weekly, *October 27, 1939*

On March 1, 1923, five years after World War I, the *Chapel Hill Weekly* began production. At the time, it cost five cents a copy.

Today, through the magic of modern technology, anyone with a computer or smartphone can view issues of the *Weekly* up to December 29, 1963. They can be accessed by logging into the Library of Congress website, chroniclingamerica.loc.gov.

Below is a sampling of snippets from the *Weekly*, selected largely at random, that transport us back to the Chapel Hill of yesteryear.

March 22, 1923: "Violets are blooming in the gardens. Hedges of spiraea along the stone walls are bursting into white....In short, spring is here. W.C. Coker, the botanist, is at the height of demand. People stop him on the street, and call him on the telephone to question him anxiously as to what and where to plant."

January 10, 1924: "The exterior of the new Carolina Inn at the west campus gate is taking its final shape."

January 22, 1925: "Josiah W. Bailey will denounce the Ku Klux Klan and Dr. W.A. Hanlett will extol it before audiences in Memorial Hall."

May 14, 1925: "A cow on the farm of Jesse Neville, who lives out to the west of Chapel Hill, went mad a few days ago and had to be killed. Mr. Neville, who had been milking her, was put under treatment for hydrophobia."

January 22, 1926: "Policeman Mack Williams, going his rounds after the hour of twelve Saturday night, saw lights in the fire company headquarters.... Coming closer, he heard noises that sounded very much like the jubilant rattling of dice, and now and again words that he was sure pertained to games of chance."

June 24, 1927: "The Murchison twins had a birthday party Tuesday."

June 8, 1928: "Chapel Hill now has a real aviation field. It is on a plateau about a mile north of the village on the left of the old Hillsboro road."

December 21, 1928: "Miss Grace Duncan and Buck Rose drew the winning number (62) in a raffle last week. The prize was the choice of a meerschaum pipe or a toilet set. Miss Duncan chose the toilet set."

June 7, 1929: "Black Bear, the celebrated pony, came to Chapel Hill on Thursday evening of last week and demonstrated his intelligence in Memorial hall....It is said that a psychologist in the Duke University faculty has been making exhaustive observations of the animal in the effort to discover the nature of his brain."

September 13, 1929: "[The Talkie] *Charming Sinners*...has been selected for the opening Vitaphone performance at the Carolina Theatre Monday."

September 27, 1929: "Default having been made in the [mortgage] payment...I will offer for sale at public auction to the highest bidder for cash, at the Post Office door in Chapel Hill, N.C., at 12:00 o'clock on Saturday, October 19, 1929...the land on which stands the original Cafeteria Building constructed by the Chapel Hill Insurance & Realty Co., and four new buildings erected by said Company on the east side of said original Cafeteria Building.—M.E. Hogan, trustee."

November 1, 1929: "The Chapel Hill citizens who trade in stocks—most of them, anyway—suffered no serious loss in the recent panic. They got out of the market while the prices were still fairly high."

August 1, 1930: "Three moonshiners deserted their still when interrupted by three of Sheriff Sloan's deputies Sunday morning, ran to the bank of Eno River, jumped in, swam across, and disappeared into the woods."

November 13, 1931: "The Red Cross, American Legion, and county welfare department have opened relief headquarters on Franklin street near the post-office through the generosity of M.E. Hogan, who has given them rent-free space for that purpose....A considerable supply of food and clothing has been stored there for distribution during the coming months."

November 18, 1932: "Members of the faculty and other persons on the University payroll face a salary cut which is expected to amount to 22 per cent for the year."

June 16, 1933: "Moths, not the troublesome clothes moths but large, beautifully-colored moths, are on view at the Ledbetter-Pickard store."

June 22, 1934: "A planting space 23 feet wide, running down the middle of North Columbia Street from the fire engine house to the North Street corner, is part of the latest improvement approved by the street committee of the board of aldermen....It will be turned over to the women of the community...and they will plant it in any way they see fit."

July 12, 1935: "The number of teachers authorized for the Chapel Hill school for the coming year remains the same as last year, 19."

June 26, 1936: "Chapel Hill is to have a new post office."

March 5, 1937: "When people in Chapel Hill awoke Sunday morning they looked out upon snow in its most beautiful aspect, not only covering the ground but also clinging to trees and shrubbery as far as the eye could see."

December 17, 1937: "The loan of an electric range and a frigidaire...has enabled the Chapel Hill high school to make a start on the organization of cooking classes."

July 15, 1938: "Leon Russell, returning to Chapel Hill after an absence of four years, says the two things about the place that make him gladdest are (1) the trees to look at and (2) the black-eyed peas to eat."

January 27, 1939: "Franklin D. Roosevelt will be 57 years old this coming Monday…and the day will be celebrated with a President's Birthday Ball at the Carolina Inn."

May 31, 1940: "Plans for homes for the University's negro janitors and other negro employees, on the old Creel place out beyond the University laundry, have progressed so far that actual construction may begin before the end of June."

November 15, 1940: "The Barbee meadow, between the Graham Memorial and the Episcopal churchyard…is being graded for a parking lot."

December 12, 1941: "Japan's attack on the United States is brought close home to Chapel Hill by the presence in Hawaii and the Philippines of members of several families here. Now that lists of casualties in Hawaii have been given out in Washington, it is assumed that persons in Hawaii who have not been heard from are safe."

December 19, 1941: "The Carolina Volunteer Training Corps has been formed by students in the University who want to be trained as soldiers for the defense of their country. Infantry drill will begin when the students come back after the holidays."

September 11, 1942: "One man was killed in an explosion in a mixing house at the munitions plant in Carrboro a few minutes before 6 o'clock Wednesday morning, and seven men were slightly injured."

February 12, 1943: "The weather turned fine Sunday, and in the bright sunshine of the afternoon people in Chapel Hill trooped to visit the new hospital of the Navy Preflight School."

May 5, 1944: "Captain J.O. Clark of the Army Air Forces, who was in the village yesterday, told of the good jobs awaiting women in the Air Transport Command."

January 5, 1945: "Coal is being rationed in small quantities to people in Chapel Hill and Carrboro, and extra supplies are being brought in through 'special directives' from the Government's Solid Fuels Administration."

November 16, 1945: "Lieutenant-Commander Howard Hamilton has come home from Japan. Mrs. Hamilton and the children were over at Durham yesterday to meet him when he stepped off the train."

November 9, 1946: "The thirty prefabricated houses allotted by the government to the Chapel Hill Veterans Housing Commission have arrived....Several of the 'demountables' are on display on a tract of land near the Horace Williams Airport."

April 18, 1947: "Tomorrow is the day for the opening of Chapel Hill's new bus station. The ceremonies will begin at 12 noon. Everyone is invited."

January 2, 1948: "Town license tags for automobiles are on sale at the Town Hall at $1."

November 18, 1949: "Most of the talk heard this week along the village streets, in stores and restaurants and barbershops, in gatherings of all sorts, has been about the wonderful time had by the people who went to New York for the Notre Dame game."

March 3, 1950: "The issuance of the new telephone directory this week gives evidence of the great expansion of Chapel Hill's telephone system. There are 42 pages of subscribers' names in this year's book as against 36 in last year's, an increase of 16 per cent."

August 17, 1951: "The records of the U.S. Weather Bureau station in Chapel Hill confirm the general impression that this summer has been an exceptionally hot one."

January 18, 1952: "Eastern Air Lines gave a preview of its splendid new Silver Falcon plane last Saturday, three days before the plane began to make its regularly scheduled flights from the Raleigh-Durham–Chapel Hill airport."

April 4, 1952: "Mrs. Ernest E. Harrill…was the winner of the electric mixer given away last week-end at the grand opening of the Dairyland Farms store in the new Glen Lennox Shopping Center."

August 7, 1953: "Throngs of people stopped at the Guy Phillips' home on East Rosemary Street until a late hour night before last to view a rare, night-blooming cereus plant in full bloom."

March 5, 1954: "The work of making over the central area of the University campus, where the Well is, began with the felling of an old oak day before yesterday."

October 29, 1954: "Congressman Carl Durham talked about atomic energy at the luncheon meeting of the Faculty Club Tuesday."

October 28, 1955: "Chapel Hill's newest retail business—Sherwin-Williams Paints—opened formally at 404 West Franklin Street yesterday.…Many persons registered yesterday…for ten prizes of steam irons or percolators."

July 13, 1956: "Grey Culbreth, the University's superintendent of utilities, has been elected Chairman of the Chapel Hill School Board."

January 4, 1957: "The Chapel Hill–Carrboro Merchants Association will have a full membership dinner meeting at Brady's on Monday night, January 14, beginning at 6:30 o'clock."

March 6, 1958: "Although the price of gasoline is lower than it was before the price war was started several weeks ago, it has risen to 30.9 cents for regular gasoline and 34.9 cents for high test gasoline."

August 13, 1959: "An ordinance aimed at putting a tight clamp on the town's two pool halls is being eyed by the Board of Aldermen."

October 10, 1960: "Aside from fogged windshields, spattered spectacles, damp clothes, squelching feet, indoor mud, soggy parcels, cancelled picnics, slow-drying laundry, cumbersome raincoats, and gluey sidewalks, the only obstacle to gracious living brought on by rainy football Saturdays in Chapel Hill is severely knotted traffic."

February 2, 1961: "The County School Board will consider the applications of 23 Negro pupils for reassignment to White Cross School, some 10 miles southeast of Chapel Hill at its meeting Monday in Hillsboro."

June 7, 1962: "The Orange County Dad's Golf Tournament registration ends tomorrow at noon."

April 24, 1963: "Army Capt. Walter W. Jackson has been assigned to the U.S. Army branch of the Military Assistance Advisory Group in Vietnam, April 9."

August 7, 1963: "A segregation protest demonstration was held in front of the University's administration building today, in the face of a warning from the UNC security officer that it would not be permitted."

November 24, 1963: "Full comprehension of President John F. Kennedy's death came slowly in Chapel Hill. All along Franklin Street, knots of people bunched around radios and television sets in stores."

December 29, 1963: "An old pep rally yell of 30 years ago was brought out of the moth balls, brushed off and decontaminated for the [upcoming] Gator Bowl:

Gator gator hoe potato
Half past alligator
Ram Bam Bulligator
Chickesaw Baw
Team! Team! Team!"

BIBLIOGRAPHY

Chapter 1: The Strowd Plantation: Past, Present and Future

Adams, Agatha Boyd. *Paul Green of Chapel Hill*. Chapel Hill: University of North Carolina Library, 1951.

Avery, Laurence G., ed. *A Southern Life: Letters of Paul Green, 1916–1981*. Chapel Hill: University of North Carolina Press, 1994.

Barrett, John G. *Sherman's March Through the Carolinas*. Chapel Hill: University of North Carolina Press, 2014.

Battle, Kemp P. *History of the University of North Carolina: From Its Beginning to the Death of President Swain, 1789–1868*. Raleigh, NC: Edwards & Broughton Printing Company, 1907.

Bryant, Bernard Lee, Jr. *Occupants and Structures of Franklin Street, Chapel Hill, North Carolina at 5-Year Intervals, 1793–1998*. Chapel Hill, NC: Chapel Hill Historical Society, 1999.

Campbell, Walter E. *Across Fortune's Tracks: A Biography of William Rand Kenan, Jr*. Chapel Hill: University of North Carolina Press, 1996.

Chapel Hill, 200 Years: Close to Magic. Chapel Hill, NC: Sheer Associates, 1994.

Conner, Fred, Pat Conner and Laura May Conner. Interview with author, April 24, 2022.

Eyre, John Douglas. *Profiles of Chapel Hill Since 1900*. Chapel Hill, NC: Chapel Hill Historical Society, 2006.

Green, Elizabeth Lay. *The Paul Green I Know*. Chapel Hill: North Caroliniana Society, 1978.

History of North Carolina: North Carolina Biography, by Special Staff of Writers. Chicago: Lewis Publishing Company, 1919.

Jesse Hargrave's Will. Orange County Wills, 1851–1868, Vol. G, 61–3.

Kenan, William R., Jr. *Incidents By the Way: Lifetime Recollections and Reflections.* N.p.: self-published, 1946.

Little, M. Ruth. *The Town and Gown Architecture of Chapel Hill, North Carolina.* Chapel Hill, NC: Preservation Society of Chapel Hill, 2006.

Long, Augustus White. "Civil War Memorandum." Wilson Special Collections Library. University of North Carolina at Chapel Hill, 1936.

———. *Son of Carolina.* Durham, NC: Duke University Press, 1939.

Margaret Hargrave's Will. Orange County Wills, 1851–1868, Vol. G, 404–5.

Orange County Deed Books, Will Books and Plat Books. Orange County, North Carolina.

Orange County Estates. "Hargrave Estate, 1866–1869." North Carolina Department of Archives and History.

Snider, William D. *Light on the Hill: A History of the University of North Carolina at Chapel Hill.* Chapel Hill: University of North Carolina Press, 1992.

Town of Chapel Hill. Minutes, Board of Aldermen Meetings. Chapel Hill, North Carolina.

Vickers, James. *Chapel Hill: An Illustrated History.* Chapel Hill, NC: Barclay Publishers, 1985.

Carolina Watchman (Salisbury, NC).

Caucasian (Raleigh, NC).

Chapel Hill Weekly.

Daily Tar Heel (Chapel Hill, NC).

Farmer and Mechanic (Raleigh, NC).

Fayetteville (NC) Observer.

Hickory (NC) Daily Record.

Hillsborough (NC) Recorder.

News & Observer (Raleigh, NC).

North Carolina Standard (Raleigh, NC).

The Review (High Point, NC).

Rockingham (NC) Post-Dispatch.

Tarborough (NC) Southerner.

Weekly Standard (Raleigh, NC).

Wilmington (NC) Journal.

Chapter 2: Professor Hedrick's Daring Stand Against Slavery

Bassett, John Spencer. *Anti-Slavery Leaders of North Carolina*. Baltimore, MD: Johns Hopkins Press, 1898.
"Gravel Wall for Houses." *Carolina Cultivator* 1, no. 12 (February 1856): 384–86.
Orange County Deed Books. Orange County, North Carolina.
Smith, Michael Thomas. *A Traitor and a Scoundrel: Benjamin Hedrick and the Cost of Dissent*. Newark, NJ: University of Delaware Press, 2003.

North Carolina Standard.

Chapter 3: Greenwood, Act 1: A Tight-Knit Collective of Artists

Adams, Agatha Boyd. *Paul Green of Chapel Hill*. Chapel Hill: University of North Carolina Press, 1951. Accessed December 26, 2021. https://digital.lib.ecu.edu/16890.
Avery, Laurence G., ed. *A Southern Life: Letters of Paul Green, 1916–1981*. Chapel Hill: University of North Carolina Press, 1994.
Daily Tar Heel. "NC Botanical Gardens to Become New Location of Paul Green Log Cabin." March 7, 1991.
Green, Elizabeth Lay. *The Paul Green I Know*. Chapel Hill: North Caroliniana Society, 1978.
Green, Paul. Interview with Jacquelyn Hall, May 30, 1975. Interview B-0005-3. Southern Oral History Program Collection (no. 4007). Accessed December 24, 2021. https://docsouth.unc.edu/sohp/html_use/B-0005-3.html.
Orange County Deed Books. Orange County, North Carolina.
Spence, James R. *Watering the Sahara: Recollections of Paul Green from 1894 to 1937*. Raleigh: North Carolina Office of Archives and History, 2008.
"A Talk by Janet Green, Given to Phi Theta Kappa, Purchase, NY, July 1981." Paul Green Foundation. Accessed December 30, 2021. https://www.ibiblio.org/paulgreen/daughter.html.
Witten, Bea. "Greenwood: Chapel Hill's Most Illustrious Neighborhood." Humanities Computing Laboratory. Accessed January 1, 2022. http://www.humancomp.org.

Chapel Hill Weekly.
Daily Tar Heel.

Henderson (NC) Daily Dispatch.
News & Observer.

Chapter 4: Mrs. Harold Walters Empowers '50s-Era Women

"Adelaide Walters Papers, 1954–1981." Wilson Special Collections Library. University of North Carolina at Chapel Hill. Accessed December 8, 2021. https://finding-aids.lib.unc.edu/04293.

Ehle, John. *The Free Men.* Lewisville, NC: Press 53, 2007.

Inter-Faith Council for Social Service. "Historical timeline." https://www.ifcweb.org/about/history, accessed 1/17/22.

———. "List of Honorees for 'A Golden Event.'" Accessed January 17, 2022. https://www.ifcweb.org.

Minutes for Meetings of the Chapel Hill Board of Aldermen.

Tribune-Press (Gouverneur, NY). "Adelaide Walters" (obituary). June 17, 1981.

Chapel Hill News Leader.
Chapel Hill Weekly.
Daily Tar Heel.
The Robesonian (Lumberton, NC).

Chapter 5: The Water Fluoridation Controversy, 1951–64

"Fluoridation Census, 1965." U.S. Department of Health, Education and Welfare. Accessed December 2, 2020. https://www.cdc.gov/fluoridation/pdf/statistics/1964.pdf.

Giduz, Roland. *Who's Gonna Cover Them Up?!: Chapel Hill Uncovered, 1950–1985.* Chapel Hill, NC: Citizen Publishing, 1985.

"A Timeline of Dental Discoveries at UNC." *North Carolina Dental Review Magazine* 24, no. 1 (Spring 2007): 6.

Town of Chapel Hill. Minutes, Meetings of the Board of Aldermen, Town of Chapel Hill, North Carolina.

Vickers, James. *Chapel Hill.* Charleston, SC: Arcadia Publishing, 1996.

Carolina Times (Durham, NC).
Chapel Hill Weekly.
Daily Tar Heel.

Chapter 6: The Desegregation Battle on the Hill

Chapman, John K. "Harold Foster—On the African American Freedom Struggle and Civil Rights Movement in Chapel Hill." Southern Historical Collection at the Louis Round Wilson Special Collections Library. Accessed February 27, 2021. https://fromtherockwall.org/oral-histories/harold-foster-on-the-african-american-freedom-struggle-and-civil-rights-movement-in-chapel-hill-part-one.

———. "Second Generation: Black Youth and the Origins of the Civil Rights Movement in Chapel Hill, NC, 1937–1963." Dissertation, University of North Carolina at Chapel Hill, 1995.

Ehle, John. *The Free Men.* Lewisville, NC: Press 53, 2007.

"Leaflet, 'Why Four People Chose Jail.'" UNC Libraries. Accessed August 12, 2022. https://exhibits.lib.unc.edu/items/show/891.

"Oral History interview with Pat Cusick, interviewed by Pamela Dean, June 19, 1989. Interview L-0043. Southern Oral History Program Collection (#4007)." Southern Historical Collection, Wilson Library, University of North Carolina at Chapel Hill.

"Oral History interview with Quinton Baker, interviewed by Chris McGinnis, February 23, 2002. Interview K-0838. Southern Oral History Program Collection (#4007)." Southern Historical Collection, Wilson Library. University of North Carolina at Chapel Hill.

Pollitt, Daniel H. "Legal Problems in Southern Desegregation: The Chapel Hill Story." *North Carolina Law Review* 43, no. 4 (June 1965): 689–767.

Sears, James T. *Lonely Hunters: An Oral History of Lesbian and Gay Southern Life, 1948–1968.* New York: Routledge, 2018.

Carolina Times (Durham, NC).
Chapel Hill Weekly.
Daily Tar Heel.
News & Observer.
The News of Orange County (Hillsborough, NC).

Chapter 7: The Room 201 Mystery

Chapel Hill Weekly.
Daily Tar Heel.
Evening Star (Washington, D.C.).
The News of Orange County.

Chapter 8: The Speaker Ban Law: Vestige of the Red Scare

"Audiocassette 83: Jesse Helms and Paul Green Conversation for Duke Filming, 10 May 1980: Side 2." The Southern Historical Collection. University Libraries. University of North Carolina. Accessed December 15, 2022. https://dc.lib.unc.edu/cdm/singleitem/collection/03ddd/id/487822/rec/2.

Avery, Laurence G., ed. *A Southern Life: Letters of Paul Green, 1916–1981.* Chapel Hill: University of North Carolina Press, 1994.

Bondurant, William, and Richard Gift, Louise Nelson, Brown Patterson, Philip Secor and Locke White. "The North Carolina Speaker Ban Law: A Study in Context." *Kentucky Law Journal* 55, issue 2, article 1. Accessed January 8, 2022. https://uknowledge.uky.edu/cgi/viewcontent.cgi?article=2896&context=klj.

Green, Paul. "The Speaker Ban Law: A Disgrace to North Carolina." Editorial. *News & Observer.* May 30, 1965.

"A Guide to the Speaker Ban Controversy at UNC-Chapel Hill, 1963–1968." Southern Oral History Program. Accessed January 8, 2022. https://sohp.org/wp-content/uploads/sites/69/2015/02/Speaker.ban_.research-guide-Feb2013.pdf.

"Interview with Daniel H. Pollitt, April 5, 1991. Interview L-0064-7. Southern Oral History Program Collection (#4007)." Documenting the American South. Accessed January 23, 2022. https://docsouth.unc.edu/sohp/playback.html?base_file=L-0064-7.

Chapel Hill Weekly.
Daily Tar Heel.
News & Observer.

Chapter 9: The Chapel Hill Weekly: Homespun News

Chapel Hill Weekly.

INDEX

About the Author

Brian Burns was born and raised in Chapel Hill. Attending UNC his freshman year, he transferred to NC State University's School of Design in 1979 to pursue a bachelor's degree in graphic design. After graduating magna cum laude in 1983, he worked as an art director for advertising agencies, including McKinney/Silver in Raleigh and the Martin Agency in Richmond. As the years passed, he doubled as a copywriter.

Brian got his first taste of history writing in 2006, as co-producer of *The Rainbow Minute* at WRIR-97.3 FM community radio in Richmond. Some episodes of the show have been broadcast worldwide.

In 2017, he published *Gilded Age Richmond* with The History Press. His previous titles include *Lewis Ginter: Richmond's Gilded Age Icon* and *Curiosities of the Confederate Capital*.

After moving to Silver Spring, Maryland, in 2015, Brian focused on his roots. Chapel Hill holds a special place in his heart. He still has family there and visits often.